Stays and Corsets Volume 2

In this second volume of *Stays and Corsets*, Mandy Barrington continues to create historical patterns for a modern body shape. This book contains all new corset patterns with a range of silhouettes that span over 300 years, from the late 16th century to the early 20th century. The corset patterns are generated from an original historical garment and have been designed for a wide range of female figures and sizes. The technique of flat pattern drafting your stays or corset will enable you to change the shape of the wearer to create an authentic historic silhouette.

All calculations have been worked out for the reader and are provided in easy-to-read tables, which avoids extremely difficult, time-consuming and inaccurate re-sizing of historical patterns. Some prior knowledge of pattern drafting is helpful; however, each pattern has step-by-step instructions supported by clear diagrams that will take you through each stage of the pattern drafting process. The final result is an accurate period stays or corset pattern for your model.

Mandy Barrington is a Senior Lecturer in Costume at the Arts University Bournemouth and a recipient of The Queen's Anniversary Prize for Higher and Further Education 2016–18. She has a first class honours degree in Costume Design and a Masters in Costume. Mandy has worked professionally making costumes for shows such as *My Fair Lady* at the National Theatre, the hit West End show *Wicked*, and *Sleeping Beauty* at The Royal Opera House, London.

Stays and Corsets Volume 2

Historical Patterns Translated for the Modern Body

Mandy Barrington

Routledge
Taylor & Francis Group

LONDON AND NEW YORK

First published 2019
by Routledge
2 Park Square, Milton Park, Abingdon, Oxon, OX14 4RN

and by Routledge
52 Vanderbilt Avenue, New York, NY 10017

Routledge is an imprint of the Taylor & Francis Group, an informa business

Library of Congress Cataloging-in-Publication Data
Barrington, Mandy.
Stays and corsets : historical patterns translated for the modern body / Mandy Barrington.
pages cm
ISBN 978-1-138-01823-5 (pbk.)—ISBN 978-1-315-77986-7 (ebook)
1. Foundation garments. 2. Corsetts—Patterns. 3. Clothing and dress measurements.
4. Vintage clothing.
I. Title. TT677.B366 2016
391.4'2—dc23
2015004096

ISBN 13: 978-1-138-06124-8 (hbk)
ISBN 13: 978-1-138-06125-5 (pbk)

Typeset in FS Albert
by Florence Production Ltd, Stoodleigh, Devon

Contents

Image credits

All technical diagrams in this book have been created by Samuel Edwards; all photographs of models in stays and corset samples have been photographed by Margaret Maguire. These two individuals have greatly contributed to the quality of the book and my ability to communicate to the reader.

Samuel Edwards at Morf
www.morfcreative.co.uk

Margaret Maguire
https://margaretmaguire.com/

I would also like to thank Hannah Hales for a selection of pattern drafting equipment illustrations and the many museums who have provided images for use in this book.

Museum collection images

1598 pair of bodies
The Bayerisches Nationalmuseum in Munich, Germany

1680–1700 ivory silk corset bodice
Russell-Cotes Art Gallery and Museum

1905 plunge front corset and *1915 deep skirted corset*
Leicestershire County Council: Symington Collection. England.

Images taken by Mandy Barrington with kind permission of the individual museum

1760 silk brocade corset bodice
The National Trust Wade Costume Collection, held at Berrington Hall

1760 strapless stays, 1830–45 buff cotton corset and *1890 Celebrated C.B. Bridal Corset*
Hampshire County Council. Provided by the Hampshire Cultural Trust.

1890 black corset
Hereford Museum Resource and Learning Centre, Hereford, England.

Acknowledgements

I would like to thank the following individuals for their very valued support in creating *Stays and Corsets: Historical Patterns Translated for the Modern Body Volume 2*. My husband Andy, family and friends who have maintained their continuous and unwavering encouragement while I have been writing this second book.

All staff and students on the BA (Hons) Costume and Performance Design course at the Arts University Bournemouth, who have greatly supported my research. In particular Katerina Lawton, Sarah Magill and Wayne Martin, who have used the patterns to teach large classes of students' pattern drafting.

Nina Horter who translated many emails from Bayerisches Nationalmuseum, Germany to help me attain a photograph of the incredible 1598 garment that forms part of their collection. Students Georgina Hoare, Imogen Howard, Hannah Rodgers, Kelly Morgan, Danielle Watkins, Ellice Thomas Bishop, Alice Frayne and Phoebe Gale for taking the time to trial my patterns before they were used on large student projects.

Individual museum staff: Gill Arnott, Keeper of the Arts, Hampshire Cultural Trust; Althea Mackenzie, curator of Hereford Museum's costume collection and the Charles Paget Wade Collection at Berrington Hall; Duncan Walker, Curator, Russell-Cotes Art Gallery & Museum; Sarah Nicol, Inspiring Collections Officer, Leicestershire County Council; and Dr. Johannes Pietsch, conservator, Bayerisches Nationalmuseum, who have all been extremely generous with their time and support.

Samuel Edwards, who has continued his commitment to high quality diagrams by painstakingly turning my roughly drawn step-by-step pattern diagrams into clear, professional illustrations. Photographer Margaret Maguire who has once again produced beautiful photographs to support the written instructions and diagrams in this book.

Chloe Pearce and Sally Boot who gave up their time to do hair and make-up on the day of the photoshoot. My models Amy Baston, Lauren Coates, Nicole Cuddihy, Sarah Magill, Katie Peachy and Poppy Wright who have supported me through the development of each corset, attending fittings, and then patiently modelling while they were photographed from every angle. All this whilst tightly laced into these restrictive garments.

Thank you all.

Introduction

I have had the opportunity to develop my passion for pattern drafting and historical clothing since writing my first book *Stays and Corsets*, examining rare and beautiful stays and corsets at museums across England. This has enabled me to further expand my knowledge and understanding of these form-fitting garments, with their ability to alter the natural shape of the wearer into what was perceived to be an ideal of beauty. Each garment studied is unique to the body it was made for and each strives to have a proportional relationship to the body it encases. Careful measuring and recording individual stays and corsets on a mannequin has revealed the importance of each garment's measurements. The correlation between these measurements creates a proportional garment that encompasses this ideal beauty.

My pattern drafting system captures the relationship of a garment to the body, this has been achieved through taking a pattern from an original historical garment and then mapping this to the same size basic block pattern (2D drawing of the body). The information gathered is used to locate the position of each panel and its correlation with the body. Therefore each pattern you draft will relate to the person you are making it for, whilst remaining historically accurate.

In this second volume of *Stays and Corsets* the patterns span over 300 years, I have recorded corsets from the late 16th century to the early 20th century. Once again, I have chosen a variety of styles and silhouettes and from these I have been able to create a whole new series of patterns, many from often unseen collections; the earliest being a 'pair of bodies' from 1598 and the latest a 'deep skirted corset' dated 1915. The stays and corsets vary greatly in shape and style; some use whalebone to stiffen the garment whilst those from the late 19th and early 20th century use steel. Full details of each original garment together with the pattern can be found at the beginning of each set of individual instructions.

There are many terms used for the tight-fitting stiffened garment that is now known as the corset. In the 16th century it was referred to as a 'pair of bodies'; later into the 17th century the term 'a pair of stays' was adopted. The word corset became commonly used during the 19th century; it derives from the French word *corps,* meaning body, and is still used today. Historical stays and corsets were designed and constructed to control the body and to alter its natural shape, producing a new silhouette. The benefit of flat pattern drafting your stays and corsets rather than cutting them in 3D on a mannequin is that you are not restricted by the contours of the mannequin. Flat pattern drafting will enable you to create a garment that will alter the shape of the wearer to the fashionable silhouette of the period.

You will begin by drafting a basic block pattern to fit your model; onto this you will transpose your chosen historical pattern. Once drafted, the basic block can be traced and used for multiple corsets. The pattern instructions follow a practical format that uses clear reference lines and number sequences to plot each panel of the new historical stays or corset. The division of the basic block, and ratio calculation for each panel of the historical garment, has been adjusted to reflect a modern body size.

Some basic prior knowledge of pattern drafting is helpful, although every stage is explained fully within the instructions. The measurements for each individual stays or corset pattern have been calculated for you and are provided in tables for each part of the body: the bust, waist and hips and for each panel of the garment. The supporting diagrams make the instructions easy to follow and the result is an accurate period garment.

I hope that through exploring the method of pattern drafting in this book you will develop your knowledge, skills and enjoyment of flat pattern drafting. I regularly use these pattern instructions to teach large groups of BA (Hons) Costume students at the Arts University Bournemouth, enabling them to successfully produce individual historical stays and corsets. The feedback received from both staff and students continues to support the further development of the pattern instructions and my understanding of the relationship of the historical garment to the body.

I wish you success in your pattern drafting endeavours and trust that this book will support the production of accurate period patterns and final garments for you or your intended wearer.

1 How to use this book

How to use this book

Guidance on the pattern drafting process

Flat pattern drafting has a long history; it can be challenging but it can also be extremely satisfying, and is one of the most accurate ways of creating a pattern for a garment. This book follows a logical sequence that begins with taking accurate measurements for your intended wearer and drafting the female basic block, and continues through to creating a new historical pattern. It is important that you read each section carefully and follow the pattern drafting process precisely. There is a glossary at the back of the book for you to refer to if there are terms that you do not understand.

Begin by collecting the equipment you need to draft your patterns; most of this is regular drawing materials, but there are some specialist items that will make the process simpler. A list is provided within the chapter on 'Pattern drafting tools'. Specialist haberdashers will stock individual items as well as pattern drafting paper.

It is extremely important that you take accurate measurements of the person for whom you will be drafting the pattern – throughout this book they will be referred to as the 'model'. The measurement guide in Chapter 3 provides information on the measurements you will need to produce all of the patterns in this book. Key information is included to support the measuring process, as well as a chart of standard measurements that you can refer to as a guide. If you are waist trained or have experience of wearing a corset you may want to be pulled in more around the waist; if this is the case I suggest that you reduce the waist measurement further and use the revised measurement for the pattern you are drafting.

All historical patterns are plotted onto a female basic block that has been drafted for your model. Once you have drafted your basic block pattern, the instructions in Chapter 5 explain how to prepare your female basic block before drafting your new historical pattern; this process is exactly the same for all patterns in the book. Once you have traced and expanded the basic block you are ready to draft a new historical stays or corset pattern.

Remember to look carefully at the diagrams contained in the book whilst drafting your historical stays and corsets as they will support the pattern you create. The pattern diagrams in this book are based on a British size 6 so the position of each line and the final shape of each panel will differ slightly depending on the size of your model. In larger sizes the position of each panel may not always fall in the same position on your female basic block pattern; use the diagrams as a guide only to help create the curves of each panel.

Once you have completed your historical pattern I recommend that you trace a second copy of your pattern, as you will then have the original to record any alterations and use again in the future. The patterns do not include a seam allowance; this is added during the cutting process and is usually 5cm at the centre back (CB) and centre front (CF) and 2.5cm on all other seams. When cutting your fabric it is important to mark the direction of the straight of grain on each pattern piece; this is parallel to the centre back and centre front lines of the original basic block pattern. These have not been indicated on the individual patterns to avoid confusion with the bone channels.

Depending on your level of experience or objectives you may want to consider which historic pattern to draft before starting. Your choice may depend on both the period of the garment and the level of difficulty. The 1890 black corset from the Hereford Museum collection is a good one to start with as it has only four panels on each side, no tricky gusset inserts and only a few bone channels. If you wish to draft an earlier corset, the 1598 'pair of bodies' example worn by Pfalzrofin Dorothea Sabina von Newburg, recorded by Nora Waugh in her book *Corsets and Crinolines*, and Janet Arnold in *Patterns of Fashion* has only two panels. Although it does have tabs these are plotted separately so are easier to draft.

In some early stays patterns I have adjusted the number of tabs and bone channels in the final garment in order to simplify it and make it more comfortable to wear; this reduction does not impact on the period silhouette. You may wish to add more bone channels to your garment; this will depend on the size of your stays or corset and the rigidity that you require. If you wish to fully bone your corset bodice

or stays, use the historical diagram at the beginning of each individual pattern instruction as a guide.

The width of bone channel varies depending on the period and style of the stays or corset. In most cases I have used between 0.7cm and 1cm wide bone channels and 1.3cm wide eyelet channels; I have placed the eyelets approximately 2.5cm apart. Your choice of boning may depend on what is available to you, so an adjustment to the bone channels on your pattern may be required to fit the new size of bone you intend to use. Information on suppliers of corset making materials is provided at the back of the book. When making your stays or corset I suggest that you fit it on your model during the early stages of construction; this valuable exercise will enable you to make adjustments to the final garment if needed.

Finding and using the measurements for your historical pattern

Each historical pattern has a series of tables of calculated measurements to enable you to draft a pattern to fit your model. Each calculated measurement will be plotted to create an individual panel, each panel is clearly numbered within the instructions for your specific stays or corset.

The measurement tables are located at the beginning of each historical pattern; these are split into parts of the body: bust, waist and hips. The measurements are separated in this way to accommodate all varieties of body shape. If your model's measurements fall between sizes within the table, choose the smaller size for the waist and the larger size for the bust and hips; the stays or corset can always be adjusted during the fitting process. The stays patterns end at the waist so only include bust and waist measurements; later corsets from 1820 onwards include hip and sometimes mid-hip, high hip or lower mid-hip measurements.

As detailed previously, the purpose of stays and corsets was to alter the silhouette of the wearer, therefore when drafting a corset or stays pattern the waist measurement is reduced to allow the waist to be pulled in and made smaller. The bust measurement is also reduced but not so dramatically, as are the hips in some patterns; this can be seen in the measurement tables. For those of you who are waist trained or wish for greater waist-reduction I suggest that you cut your waist measurement further and use the measurements from the chart for the size smaller.

Gather and record the measurements for your model and create an individual table of panel sizes for the pattern you are drafting. The full measurement closest to your model is in the column on the far left, the half measurement and half reduced measurement will be listed next to it, the resulting calculations for each panel are listed below the individual panel number.

You can check the key measurements of your pattern once drafted by adding up the width of each panel from the centre back (CB) to the centre front (CF) on the bust, waist and hip lines. This should total your half reduced measurement for each part of the body.

The diagram below gives an example of an individual measurement table and how to use the table to find the specific measurements referred to within the pattern instructions.

Example:

Begin plotting the 1760 corset bodice pattern onto your traced female basic block.

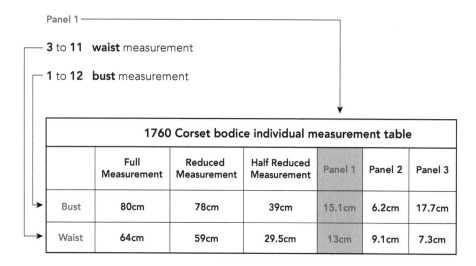

Panel 1

3 to 11 **waist** measurement

1 to 12 **bust** measurement

1760 Corset bodice individual measurement table						
	Full Measurement	Reduced Measurement	Half Reduced Measurement	Panel 1	Panel 2	Panel 3
Bust	80cm	78cm	39cm	15.1cm	6.2cm	17.7cm
Waist	64cm	59cm	29.5cm	13cm	9.1cm	7.3cm

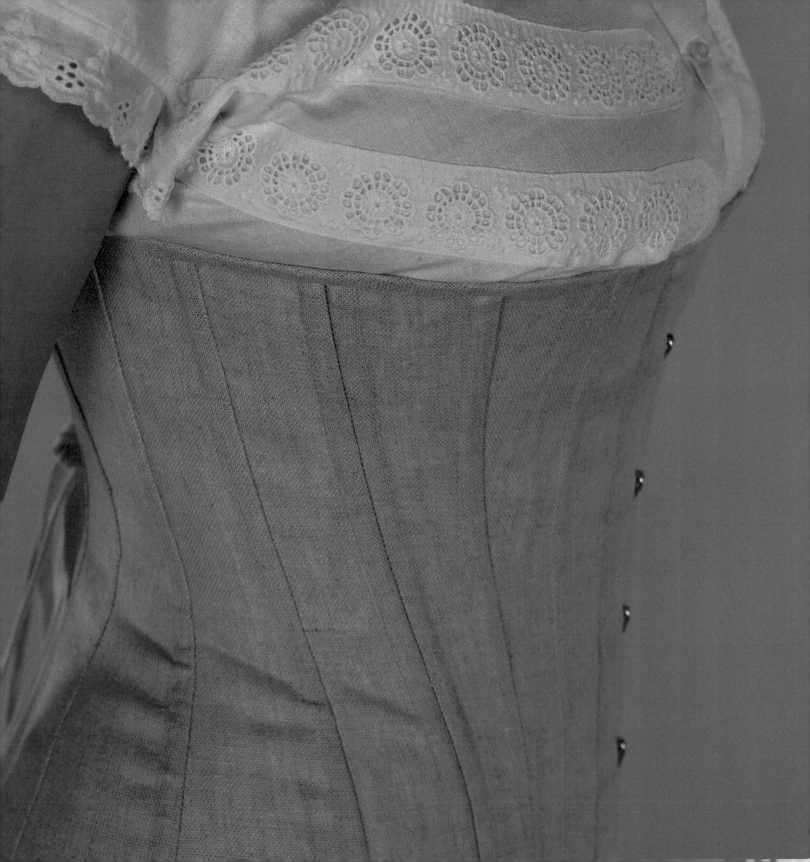

2 Pattern drafting tools

Pattern drafting tools

Since writing my first book the number of specialist pattern drafting tools on the market has continued to increase, although most are regular drawing and measuring equipment. I have listed the tools that are useful for the whole pattern drafting process, from taking measurements of your model to drawing up your patterns. Specialist equipment such as a Pattern Master or similar grading rule, set square and a hip/ tailor's curve are particularly beneficial for the process of producing accurate patterns and smooth curves. As the pattern instructions use metric measurements, metric tools would simplify this process and avoid converting the measurements to imperial.

Pattern paper comes in various widths usually on a roll – can be plain or may be marked with a grid or spot; the paper is strong but relatively thin and should be suitable for tracing.

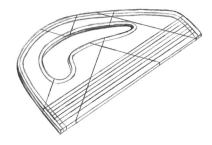

Pattern Master – a multi-purpose drawing aid designed to assist with pattern drafting – it incorporates useful curves, measurements and angles.

Ruler and metre rule for measuring and drawing lines.

French curve – a tool for drawing different shaped curves.

Flexible ruler – a flexible drawing tool for curves.

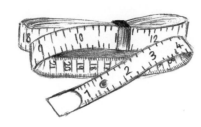

Tape measure – a flexible tape with centimetres and/ or inches used to measure the person for whom you will be drafting your pattern (your model).

Calculator – essential for calculating measurements throughout the pattern drafting process.

Pattern wheel – a tool for tracing through patterns.

Scissors – a tool for cutting your pattern once traced.

Cotton tape – use to place around your model's waist and hips whilst taking measurements.

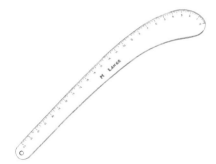

Hip curve or tailors curve – a curved ruler that can be used to create long graceful curves when pattern drafting.

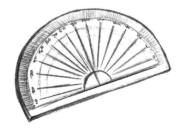

Protractor – a tool for measuring angles.

Sharp pencil – it is important to use a sharp pencil to keep your lines precise and neat.

3 Female measurements

Female measurements

To translate the three dimensional shape of the body into a two dimensional pattern you need to use the body's measurements as a guide. The following section will support you gathering the measurements that you require to draft the female basic block.

Correct measurements form the basis for accurate pattern drafting; taking precise measurements is extremely important as they will enable you to draft a basic block pattern to the size of your model. The measurements you will need are included in the table opposite; guidance for taking these measurements is provided on the following pages. Look carefully at the measurement diagrams and read each description for the position of the related measurement. Complete a personal table with your model's measurements before drafting your female basic block pattern.

Watch points when taking measurements

It is very easy to take inaccurate measurements; take extra care when measuring your model, as incorrect measurements will dramatically alter your basic block pattern and affect the accuracy of the new historical pattern you will plot onto your basic block. I suggest that you place a tape around the **waist** and leave it there whilst taking all measurements.

The **nape** to **waist** and **waist** to **hip** measurement is most often recorded incorrectly, resulting in the length of the pattern being too short. As a guide the **nape** to **waist** measurement is generally around **41cm** long, with a tolerance of up to **2cm** either side of that measurement for someone who is taller or shorter; this will also depend on the proportion of your person. An average **waist** to **hip** measurement is **20cm** again with a tolerance of up to **2cm**. A **mid-hip** measurement is half this measurement, being approximately **10cm** below the **waist**.

Standard female measurements are also provided to help you check those you have taken from your model. It is unlikely that these will correspond exactly to the standard sizes but will enable you to make a comparison to those you have gathered to see if you have taken a wildly inaccurate measurement in error. In addition to the measurements you take, an observation of the person measured, in respect of stance and figure, is also beneficial. This will describe details that measurements alone will not capture and will help you when drafting your patterns. For example, the model may have sloping **shoulders** or a large **bust** in comparison to the **waist**. Record these on your measurement form in the section "additional information".

Female Measurement Form for Drafting the Female Basic Block

Name		Date	
Bust		**Nape to Waist Back** (approx **41cm** down from the nape)	
Under Bust		**Waist to Hip** (approx **20cm** down from the waist)	
Waist		**Across Back**	
Mid-Hip (approx **10cm** down from the waist)		**Across Chest**	
Hip		**Point to Point**	
Neck		**Dart Size**	

Additional Information

Female Measurement Guide

Area of Body	How to take the measurement
Bust	Measure horizontally around the fullest part of the **bust**
Under Bust	Measure horizontally around the torso directly under the **bust**
Waist	Measure horizontally around the thinnest part of the torso, above the **hip** bones. Fasten a cotton tape around the **waist** while taking further measurements
Hip	Taken horizontally around the fullest area of the **seat**, with the feet together. Fasten a cotton tape around the **hip** while taking further measurements
Mid-Hip	A **mid-hip** measurement is taken **10cm** below the **waist** or at the halfway point between the **waist**line and the **hip** line. Measure horizontally around the body
Nape to Waist (Back)	Measure from the first prominent bone at the base of the **neck** down to the waist. Use the tape around the **waist** as a guide and ensure that your model is standing upright and looking forward while you take the measurement
Waist to hip	Measure down from the **waist** to the **hip** at the side of the body (this measurement is usually between **20cm** and **22cm**). Use a tape around the **waist** and the **hip** as a guide
Across Back	The narrowest distance from the crease of each **armhole** when down. This measurement is above the **bust** line across the **shoulder** blades
Across Chest	The narrowest distance from the crease of each **armhole** when down. This measurement is above the **bust** line
Point to Point	The measurement between the most prominent part of each **breast** (usually between **15cm** and **20cm**)
Neck	Measure around the base of the **neck**

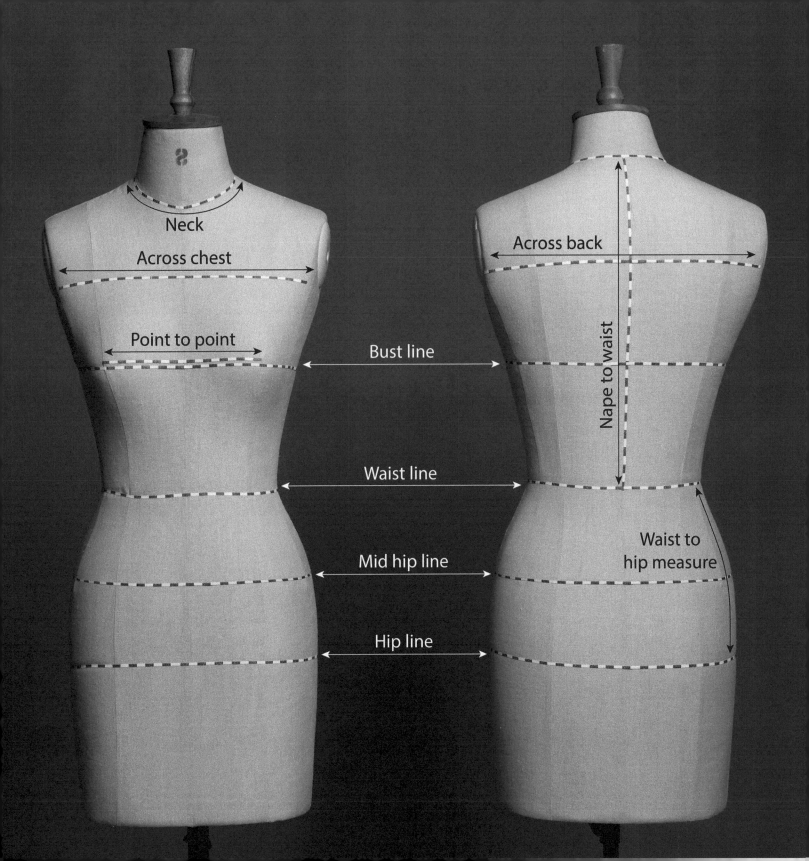

Neck

Across chest

Point to point

Bust line

Waist line

Mid hip line

Hip line

Across back

Nape to waist

Waist to hip measure

Female measurement table

The measurements in the table below are based on British sizing, but have been supported and adapted through the collection of measurements from a large group of female models. These can be used to create your basic block pattern, or as a guide when taking your own measurements from your model. Each person has a unique body shape so these measurements are unlikely to match your model exactly. All measurements are recorded in centimetres and are for a person of average height 160cm to 170cm.

Taking your own measurements using the information provided is by far the most precise way of creating an accurate basic block pattern. If you are unsure about any of the measurements you are taking from your model the Female Standard Measurement Table will provide an example of a standard measurement for the size.

Female Standard Measurement Table

	6	8	10	12	14	16	18	20	22	24
Bust	80	82	86	90	94	100	106	112	118	124
Under Bust	68	70	74	78	82	86	90	96	102	108
Waist	62	64	68	72	76	82	88	94	100	104
Mid-Hip	80	84	88	92	96	100	106	112	118	124
Hip	84	88	92	96	100	106	112	118	124	130
Across Back	32	33	34	35	36	37	38	39	40	41
Nape to Waist	38.5	39	39.5	40	40.5	41	41.5	42	42.5	43
Across Chest	29	30	31	32.5	33.5	35	36.5	38	39	40.5
Point to Point	17	18	19	20	21	22	22.5	23	24	25
Waist to Hip	20	20	20.5	20.5	21	21	21.5	21.5	22	22
Neck	35	35	36	36	37	38	39	40	40	40

4 The female basic block

The female basic block

The female basic block pattern uses the measurements taken from your model to create a pattern that will fit closely to the torso, providing a 2D drawing of the bodies' 3D shape. This basic block pattern is unique to the individual you are drafting for and can be adapted to create many other patterns. Drafting an accurate female basic block pattern for your model will provide a foundation for your historical pattern drafting.

To draft your female basic block pattern follow both the written instructions and diagrams throughout the drafting process. The proportion of your basic block pattern should closely resemble the diagrams provided, but may differ slightly to the example in this book as the proportional measurements of your model are individual. For example the position of the bust dart will depend on the size of the model's bust, the amount of side seam suppression will depend on the size of the waist.

Take care at certain points during the drafting process. The position of the key lines, **bust**, **waist** and **hips** are crucial to a proportional pattern; make sure these are located in the correct position. When plotting your pattern always measure from the first number that is indicated in the instructions, for example **1** to **6** is **2cm**; measure from point **1** to find point **6**. Complete your table of measurements before beginning; a copy of this is provided within the chapter 'Female measurements' for you to photocopy. Mark your pattern with the letters and numbers provided as you draft them and label each key line as shown for additional guidance.

Female basic block instructions

Take accurate measurements of your model using the guidelines provided in the measurement section of the book. Record these before beginning to draft your female basic block.

Calculate the proportional measurements required to draft the female basic block:

Half Bust	Nape to Waist (back)	Half Across Chest
Half Waist	Waist to Hip	Half Point to Point
Half Hip	Half Across Back	One Fifth Neck

Measurements required to draft the female basic block

Bust	Nape to Waist (back)	Across Chest
Waist	Waist to Hip	Point to Point
Hip	Across Back	Neck

Standard dart sizes

Bust	80cm	82cm	86cm	90cm	94cm	100cm	106cm	112cm	118cm	124cm
Dart	6.3cm	6.4cm	6.8cm	7.2cm	7.6cm	8.8cm	9cm	9.7cm	10.6cm	11.3cm

Draw a rectangle in which the female basic block will be drawn

A to **B**   half **bust** measure plus **2.5cm**

A to **C**   (**nape** to **waist back** measure plus **2.5**) plus **waist** to **hip** measure (this is the **Centre Back** (**CB**) line)

B to **D**   equal to (**A** to **C**) measure (this is the **Centre Front** (**CF**) line)

C to **D**   equal to (**A** to **B**) measure (this is the **hip** line)

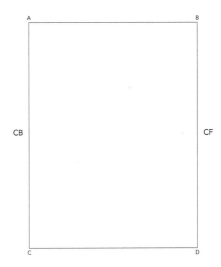

Female basic block back

A to 1	**2.5cm back neck** (nape) point
1 to 2	**nape** to **waist** measure
2 to 3	square across from **CB** to **CF** (**waist**line)
1 to 4	half measurement (**1** to **2**) plus **1.3cm**
4 to 5	square across from **CB** to **CF** (**bust** line)
1 to 6	half measurement (**1** to **4**)
6 to 7	square across half **across back** measure (**across back** line)
1 to 8	half measurement (**1** to **6**) minus **2cm**

8 to 9	square across half **across back** measure plus **1.5cm** (**across shoulder** line)
7 to 10	square up to **shoulder** line
7 to 11	square down to **bust** line
4 to 12	half measurement (**4** to **5**) minus **1.3cm**
12 to 13	square down to the **hip** line
1 to 14	one fifth **neck** measure
14 to 15	square up **1.3cm**
1 to 15	connect with a deep concave curve
15 to 9	connect with a straight line

11 to 16	draw a **2cm** line at a **45** degree angle to line (**11** to **12**). This is a guide only for the position and shape of your front **armhole**, the angle of the curve will depend on the size of your pattern.

9 through **7** and **16** to **12** connect with a concave curve (this is the back **armhole**)

Note: Using a Pattern Master, tailors curve or French curve will help to create a smooth continuous line for the **armhole**

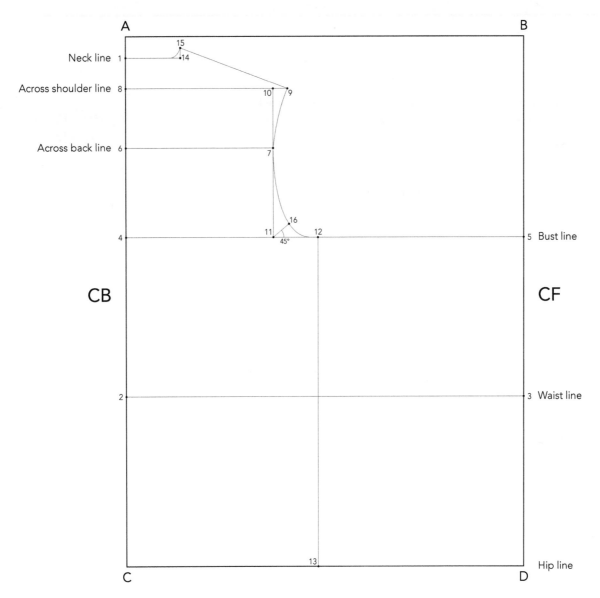

A   B

Neck line   1

15
14

Across shoulder line   8

10   9

Across back line   6

7

16

11   12
45°

4   5   Bust line

CB   CF

2   3   Waist line

13

Hip line

C   D

Female basic block front neck and shoulder

Female basic block front neck and shoulder

5 to **17**	one tenth **nape** to **waist** (back) measurement taken from your pattern between points (**1** to **2**)
B to **18**	one fifth **neck** measure minus **0.7cm**
B to **19**	one fifth **neck** measure plus **3cm**
18 to **19**	connect the two **neck** points with a straight line
B to **20**	draw a line at a **45** degree angle to line (**B** to **18**) to meet line (**18** to **19**)
20 to **21**	extend line **B** to **20** by **1.5cm** to find point **21**

18 through **21** to **19** connect with a concave curve (this is the **front neck**)

18 to **22**	**shoulder** length (**15** to **9**) minus **0.6cm** taken from your pattern
22 to **23**	square down **5cm**. This provides the position and angle of the front **shoulder**.

Find your individual dart size from the table at the beginning of the instructions or calculate the size of your dart using the formula provided

18 through **23** to **24 shoulder** length (**15** to **9**) plus your individual dart size

5 to **25**	half **point** to **point** measure
25 to **26**	square up to the **shoulder** line
25 to **27**	to **28** square down to the **waist**line and **hip** line

---

Calculating your dart size

(three fifths **bust** measure minus **across chest** measure)
divided by **3**
= **dart size**

Example: 78cm bust

three fifths **bust** = **46.8cm**
across chest = **29.5cm**

46.8cm minus **29.5cm** = **17.3cm**
divided by **3**

Total dart size = **5.8cm**

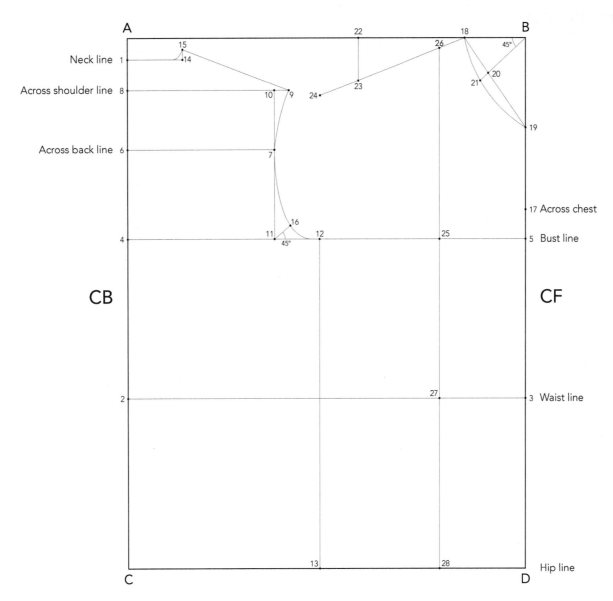

A

22   18   B

15   26   45°

Neck line   1   14

20

23   21

Across shoulder line   8   10   9   24

19

Across back line   6   7

17 Across chest

16

4   11   12   25   5   Bust line

45°

CB   CF

2   27   3   Waist line

13   28   Hip line

C   D

Female basic block front bust dart and armhole

25 to **29**	2.5cm
26 to **30**	2cm
30 to **29**	connect with a straight line
30 to **31**	**Bust Dart Size**

Note: The position of your dart (**30** to **31**) may be closer to guideline (**22** to **23**) or for larger bust sizes may fall just the other side of point **23**.

Measure line **30** to **29** transfer this measurement to create line **29** through **31** to find point **32**

Ensure line (**30** to **29**) is the same length as line (**29** to **32**)

31 to **33**	half measurement (**31** to **30**)
33 to **34**	square up at a **90** degree angle from line **30** to **31** to hit line **A** to **B**
24 to **35**	connect **24** through the top of point **32** to find point **35** on line (**33** to **34**)
35 to **30**	connect with a straight line

17 to **36** and **37**	square across from point **17** to the dart to find points **36** and **37**
17 to **38**	half **across chest** measure plus measurement between points (**36** to **37**) draw a line from **17** through **36** and **37** to find point **38**. Therefore (**17** to **37**) plus (**36** to **38**) equals half the across **chest** measure
38 to **39**	square down to the **bust** line
39 to **40**	draw a **2cm** line at a **45** degree angle to line (**38** to **39**).

This is a guide only for the position and shape of your back **armhole**, the angle of the curve will depend on the size of your pattern.

24 through **38** and **40** to **12** connect with a concave curve (this is the **front armhole**)

The basic block without the waist darts and side seam suppression is now ready to adapt into the stays and corset patterns.

The instructions on the following pages will enable you to add waist darts and the waist and hip position to your female basic block. The basic block with darts can be adapted to create patterns for other garments.

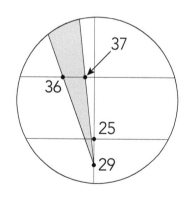

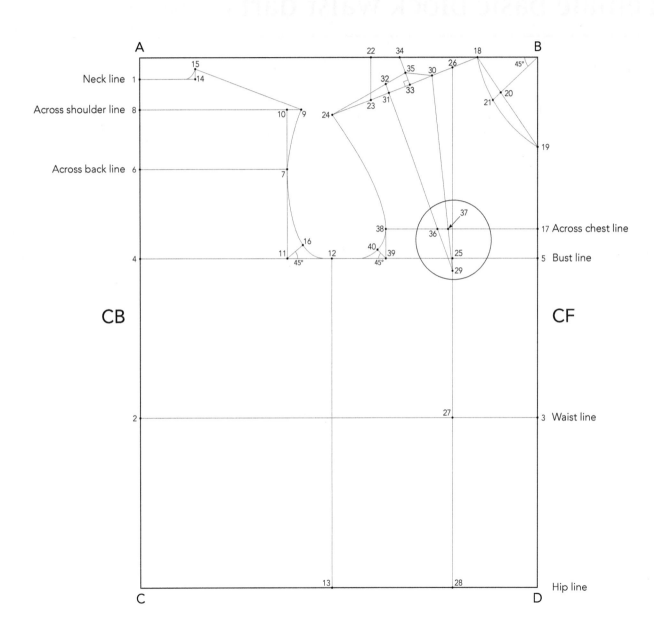

A

B

Neck line 1

15

14

Across shoulder line 8

10 9

Across back line 6

7

4

16

11

45°

12

38

40 39

45°

24

22 34

32

35 30

33

23 31

26

18

45°

20

21

19

37

36 25

29

17 Across chest line

5 Bust line

CB

CF

2

27

3 Waist line

13

28

Hip line

C

D

Female basic block waist darts

Back

4 to **41**	half measurement (**4** to **11**) square down to **waist**line **42** and **hip** line **43**
42 to **44**	two thirds measurement (**2** to **C**) **waist** to **hip**
42 to **45**	1cm
42 to **46**	1cm

41 to **45** to **44** and
41 to **46** to **44** connect with straight lines to make the **back dart**

Front

29 to **47**	3cm
27 to **48**	one third measurement (**2** to **C**) **waist** to **hip**
27 to **49**	1.5cm
27 to **50**	1.5cm

47 to **49** to **48** and
47 to **50** to **48** connect with straight lines to make the **front dart**

Waist distribution calculation

(half **waist** measurement plus ease **2.5cm**)

divided by **2**
= total

Back waist distribution: **total** minus **1.3cm**
Front waist distribution: **total** plus **1.3cm**

Example: half **waist** measurement **= 32.5cm**

Back: $\dfrac{(32.5\text{cm plus }2.5\text{cm}) = 17.5\text{cm minus }1.3\text{cm} = 16.2\text{cm}}{2}$

Front: $\dfrac{(32.5\text{cm plus }2.5\text{cm}) = 17.5\text{cm plus }1.3\text{cm} = 18.8\text{cm}}{2}$

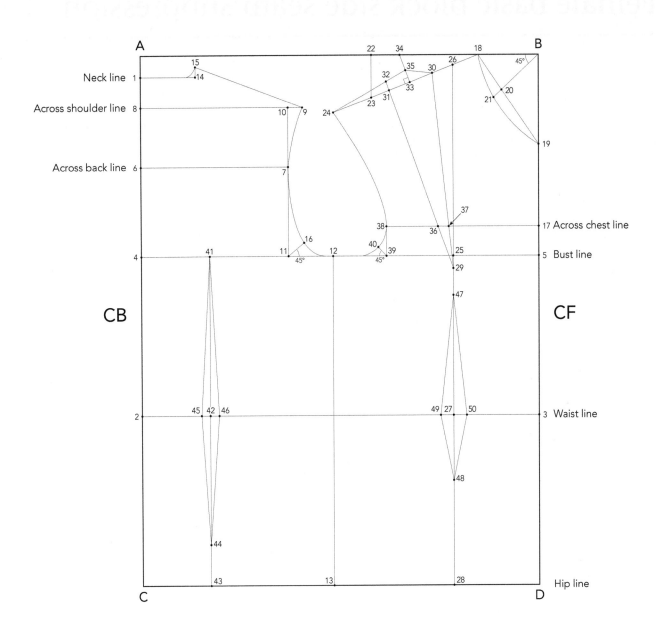

Female basic block side seam suppression

Waist distribution

2 to **51**	back **waist** calculation plus **2cm** for back dart (**45** to **46**)
3 to **52**	front **waist** calculation plus **3cm** for front dart (**50** to **49**)
12 to **51**	connect with a straight line
12 to **52**	connect with a straight line

Hip distribution

C to **53**	back **hip** calculation
D to **54**	front **hip** calculation
51 to **53**	connect with a gentle convex curve
52 to **54**	connect with a gentle convex curve

Note: The front and back hip lines should overlap unless the waist is large in relation to the hips.

Once you have finished your darts and side seam suppression your female basic block is complete.

Hip distribution calculation

(half **hip** measurement plus ease **2.5cm**)
divided by **2**

= total
Back hip distribution: **total** minus **1.3cm**
Front hip distribution: **total** plus **1.3cm**

Example: half **hip** measurement = **45cm**

Back: (45cm plus **2.5cm**) = **23.75cm** minus **1.3cm** = **22.45cm**
　　　　　2

Front: (45cm plus **2.5cm**) = **23.75cm** plus **1.3cm** = **25.05cm**
　　　　　2

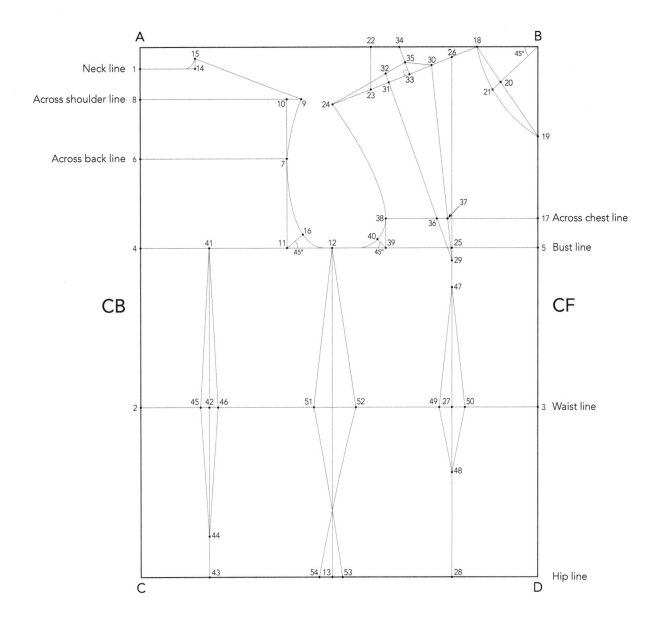

A   B

Neck line   1

Across shoulder line   8

Across back line   6

17 Across chest line

5   Bust line

CB   CF

2   3   Waist line

Hip line

C   D

5 Preparing the female basic block for your historic pattern

Preparing the female basic block for your historic pattern

Once you have chosen the pattern you wish to draft, the first stage is to trace and separate the front and back of the completed female basic block (without **waist** darts). This same process should be followed for all of the pattern instructions in this book. Label each line as shown in the diagrams, but **do not** transfer the numbers from your original female basic block. Your pattern paper should be large enough for you to separate your female basic block pattern, **100cm × 90cm** should be sufficient for sizes up to **106cm**, sizes above **106cm** will need paper **120cm × 100cm.** You will require a larger piece of paper for the 1915 Deep Skirted Corset due to its longer length; **160cm × 90cm** should be sufficient for sizes up to **106cm,** sizes above **106cm** will need paper **180cm × 100cm.**

Draw additional guidelines onto your pattern paper

Draw a vertical line **10cm** from the left-hand edge of your paper, this is a guide for your new centre back (**CB**) line. Draw a horizontal line across the width of

your paper **30cm** up from the bottom edge. This line is a guide for your new **waist**line. For the 1915 corset draw a line **60cm** up from the bottom edge.

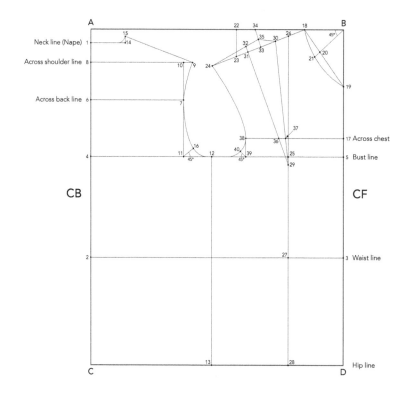

Trace the back of your female basic block

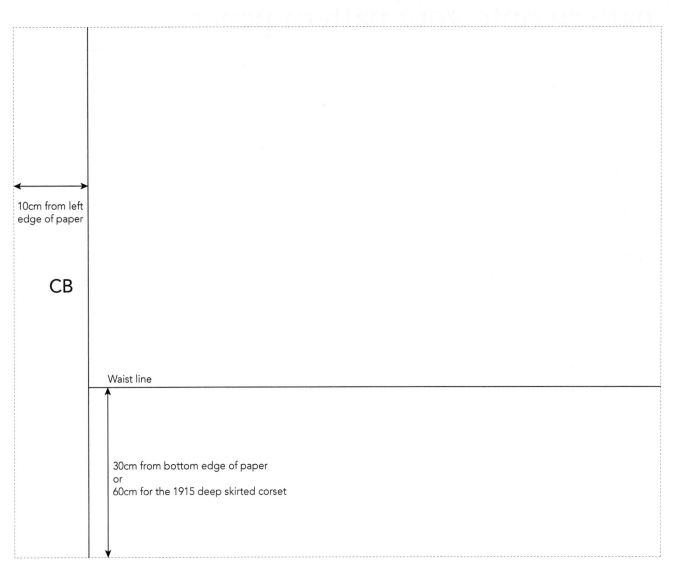

CB

10cm from left
edge of paper

Waist line

30cm from bottom edge of paper
or
60cm for the 1915 deep skirted corset

Trace the back of your female basic block pattern onto your pattern paper

Begin by matching the centre back (**CB**) of your female basic block pattern with your new centre back line on your pattern paper. Ensure the **waist**line also lies on the new **waist**line on your pattern paper.

Trace the back of your female basic bock onto your pattern paper, omitting lines (**10** to **11**), (**11** to **16**). Square across from the **CB** line to extend the **bust** line and **hip** line to the same length as the **waist** guideline.

In order to accommodate the new historical pattern a gap is needed between the back and front of the female basic block. The size of this gap will depend on the individual historical pattern you are drafting.

On the bust line of your traced pattern mark a point **25cm** or **30cm** from the back side seam of the traced female basic block. The information on the size of gap needed is provided with the individual

historical pattern instructions. Square down from this point to the **waist**line and **hip** line. This is the new side seam for the front of the female basic block.

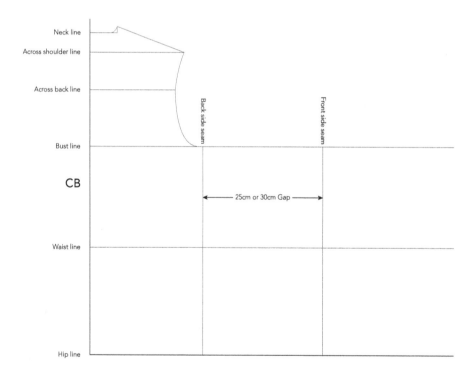

Trace the front of your female basic block pattern onto your pattern paper

Match the front side seam of your female basic block with the new side seam on your pattern paper; ensure that the **waist**line, **bust** line and **hip** line also lie on the new lines that you have drawn on your pattern paper. Trace the front of your basic bock onto your pattern paper omitting additional guidelines, at the neck (**18** to **19**) and (**B** to **21**), at the shoulder (**26** to **28**), (**22** to **23**) and (**33** to **34**), at the armhole (**38** to **39**) and (**39** to **40**); see basic block diagram.

Line **C**   on the **bust** line measure half the distance between the newly traced female basic block back side seam and new female basic block front side seam, square down to the **waist**line and **hip** line.

Number and label the following lines on your new traced female basic block

1 to 2   **bust** line
3 to 4   **waist**line
5 to 6   **hip** line

Your female basic block pattern is now prepared for your historical pattern drafting.

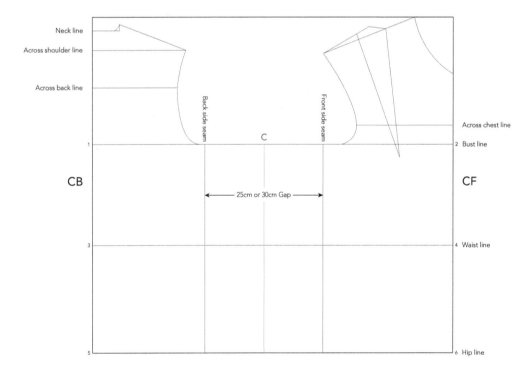

6 Historical patterns

Historical patterns

Introduction

My continued studies into stays and corsets have revealed many examples of corsets made by the professional stay maker or corsetiere, as well as those that have been lovingly handmade at home to replicate the fashionable shapes of the period. These garments reflect the wide range of women's body shapes across the centuries, emphasising our individuality and uniqueness. The stays and corset examples in museums are often bespoke so therefore do not necessarily follow strict rules on shape and construction. Many have taken on the figure of the owner through constant wear and reveal information about their status as well as their body shape.

Favourite stays were often mended, patched and even adapted, the outer fabric reflecting the new fashionable shape whilst the structured and fully boned foundation stayed the same. This is not so common with later corsets, maybe due to new manufacturing processes which altered how they were constructed and in turn the cost. Dating stays and corsets can sometimes be difficult as they were often worn outside the dates recorded by the museum; within one decade a range of styles would have been worn.

The bespoke nature of the corset began to change in the 19th century when some standard sizing was introduced in corsets that were manufactured. The development of the ready-to-wear market included the corset, which became available to buy across the counter in a high street store. The shape of corsets became more uniform and advertisements in ladies' periodicals encouraged women to purchase the new designs available for the fashionable silhouette of the period. The desire to have a small waist continued; this perception of beauty has persisted through centuries from the earliest examples of corsetry to the most recent, sometimes achieved by the most extreme tight lacing.

Female body shapes today are proportionally very different to those prior to the 20th century, when controlling foundation garments were worn from early childhood. This practice helped to develop a straight back and a small waist, altering the posture and natural proportions of the body. The historical patterns in this book have been developed for the modern body shape, and where necessary have been adapted to create the same panel shapes and final silhouette as the original historical garment.

The information gathered from examining historic stays and corsets has not only supplied measurements and proportions for each pattern in this book but has also provided valuable information on each garment's construction and alteration. This is detailed in each individual pattern chapter.

7 1598 'pair of bodies'

1598 'pair of bodies'

This very rare garment known as a 'pair of bodies' or a corset is held at the Bayerisches Nationalmuseum, Munich, Germany. The corset is dated 1598, was originally worn by Pfalzrofin Dorothea Sabina von Newburg and was recovered from her tomb at Lavingen. It is made from fine corded silk and is hand stitched throughout. The original colour of the garment is thought to have been ivory but has now discoloured to a yellow beige. The garment is extremely fragile and the original lining and interlining along with the whalebone and other stiffening have not survived. This corset is thought to be the earliest surviving garment of its type and is now so fragile that it can no longer be displayed at the museum.

The 'pair of bodies' is small with a waist measurement of 53.2cm (21 inches) and bust measurement of only 78.7cm (31 inches). The centre front is 35.5cm (14 inches) and the centre back is 24.7cm (9.75 inches). It has two back panels, a front panel and two straps; it also has six tabs that are stab stitched to the hemline of the corset and eyelet holes where a farthingale would have been tied in place. The back panel has boning channels either side of the eyelet channel; the eleven eyelet holes either side are hand sewn over metal rings. The lines of stitching on the front panel are shaped under the bust. This early corset created a very conical body shape and flat bust. The garment would have been worn under a bodice to provide the historical silhouette of the period

These 1598 'pair of bodies' have been recorded by Janet Arnold in *Patterns of Fashion* and by Norah Waugh in her book *Corsets and Crinolines*. A comparison of these patterns reveals differences to the shaping particularly around the armhole. I have chosen to use Norah Waugh's diagram within my book.

The 1598 corset pattern is relatively simple to draft and produces an authentic period silhouette. It has a wide front panel and two narrow back panels. The tabs are drafted separately and applied once the main garment is constructed. The strap is also drafted as a separate piece; this helps at the fitting stage to create the right shape and angle across the shoulder. The final pattern has the same number of bones as the original along with the front shaping; this provides an accurate corset for the period. If you wish to adapt this to a period bodice, omit the shaping around the bust and replace with full length bones in the front panel. The two back panels have very little bones – more can be added for larger sizes.

Opposite: 1598 'pair of bodies' of lightweight finely corded silk worn by Pfalzrofin Dorothea Sabina von Newburg.

Bayerisches Nationalmuseum, Munich, Germany.

Original 1598 'pair of bodies' pattern

The lines on the 1598 historical pattern diagram opposite are a guide for drafting the new pattern onto the female basic block. The approximate position of the **bust** line and **waist**line are shown on the diagram; it is also labelled with the **CB** and **CF** and line **C** as an additional guide.

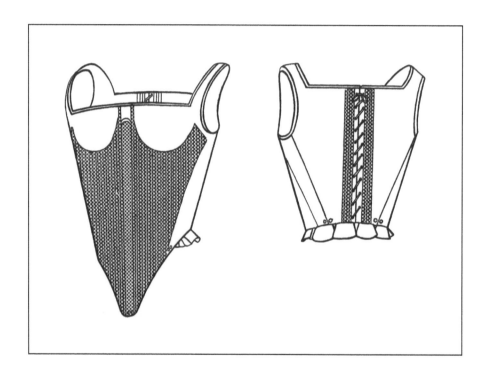

Body of yellow-brown silk, front and back diagrams showing the position of the bone channels. From *Corsets and Crinolines* by Norah Waugh.

Opposite: Body of yellow-brown silk pattern diagram from *Corsets and Crinolines* by Norah Waugh with additional guidelines for the placement of the bust and waist.

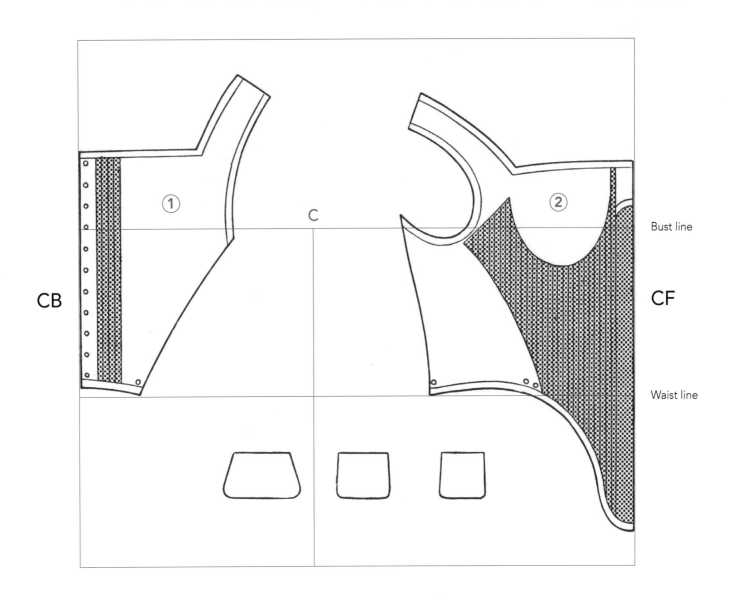

CB

CF

C

Bust line

Waist line

①

②

Guidelines for the 1598 'pair of bodies' pattern

Trace and separate the female basic block pattern following the instructions in Chapter 5, 'Preparing the female basic block for your historic pattern'. Leave a gap of **25cm** between the basic block back side seam and basic block front side seam, and number each line.

Draw in the following additional guidelines

7 to **8**   **mid-hip** line

The **mid-hip** line lies half measurement (**3** to **5**) square across from the **CB** line to the **CF** line

9 to **10**   **across back** line
11 to **12** **across chest** line

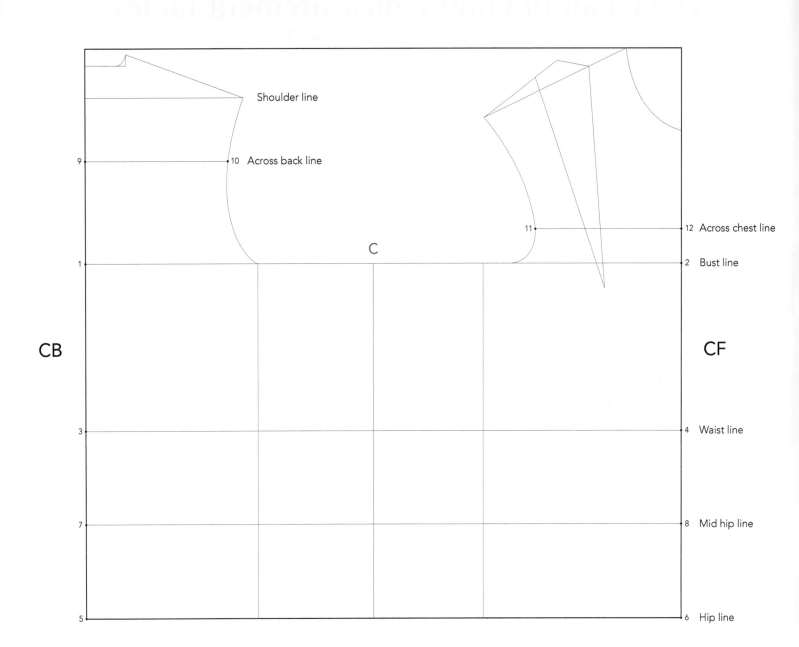

Shoulder line

9   10   Across back line

C

11   12   Across chest line

1   2   Bust line

CB   CF

3   4   Waist line

7   8   Mid hip line

5   6   Hip line

1598 'pair of bodies' measurement tables

The tables below contain measurements for each pattern piece. Find the **bust** and **waist** measurements that are the closest to that of your model. The calculation for the size of each panel is recorded horizontally to these measurements.

1598 pair of bodies measurement table for the bust

Bust measurement	Reduced bust measurement	Half reduced bust measurement	Panel 1	Panel 2
80cm	78cm	39cm	15.5cm	23.5cm
82cm	80cm	40cm	16cm	24cm
86cm	84cm	42cm	16.5cm	25.5cm
90cm	88cm	44cm	17cm	27cm
94cm	92cm	46cm	18cm	28cm
100cm	98cm	49cm	19cm	30cm
106cm	104cm	52cm	20cm	32cm
112cm	110cm	55cm	21cm	34cm
118cm	116cm	58cm	22cm	36cm
124cm	122cm	61cm	24cm	37cm

1598 pair of bodies measurement table for the waist

Full waist measurement	Reduced waist measurement	Half reduced waist measurement	Panel 1	Panel 2
62cm	57cm	28.5cm	7cm	21.5cm
64cm	59cm	29.5cm	7.5cm	22cm
68cm	63cm	31.5cm	8cm	23.5cm
72cm	67cm	33.5cm	8.5cm	25cm
76cm	71cm	35.5cm	9cm	26.5cm
82cm	77cm	38.5cm	9.5cm	29cm
88cm	83cm	41.5cm	10.5cm	31cm
94cm	89cm	44.5cm	11.5cm	33cm
100cm	95cm	47.5cm	12.5cm	35cm
104cm	99cm	49.5cm	13.5cm	36cm

Create a table of measurements for your model

Create an individual table for your model
to isolate the specific measurements
required to draft your historical pattern.
See example table below.

1598 pair of bodies individual measurement table example

Size	Full measurement	Reduced measurement	Half reduced measurement	Panel 1	Panel 2
Bust	80cm	78cm	39cm	15.5cm	23.5cm
Waist	64cm	59cm	29.5cm	7.5cm	22cm

Begin plotting panel 1 of the 1598 'pair of bodies' onto your traced basic block pattern

Panel 1

3 to **13**	**waist** measurement
1 to **14**	**bust** measurement
14 to **15**	square up **1.5cm** to find point **15**
15 to **13**	connect with a temporary straight line

9 to **16**	**1.3cm** on **CB** line
16 to **17**	square across from point **16** with a temporary line to **0.3cm** beyond the basic block back **armhole** to find point **17**
17 to **18**	one quarter measurement (**16** to **17**) plus **0.6cm**

18 to **19**	square up from point **18** with a temporary line to the **shoulder** line to find point **19**
19 to **20**	**1.5cm** on line (**18** to **19**)
20 to **21**	square across from point **20** with a temporary line to the basic block back **armhole** to find point **21**

20 to **22**	one third measurement (**20** to **21**)
22 to **18**	connect with a straight line
22 to **23**	draw a line one quarter measurement (**9** to **10**) **across back** line – at a **90** degree angle to line (**18** to **22**)

23 through **17** to **15** connect with a shallow concave curve to create the new back **armhole**

16 to **24**	**0.3cm** on the **CB** line
24 to **18**	connect with a very slight convex curve

3 to **25**	**1cm** on the **CB** line
25 to **13**	connect with a shallow concave curve

13 to **26**	half measurement (**13** to **15**)
26 to **27**	square across **0.6cm**

15 through **27** to **13** connect with a shallow concave curve

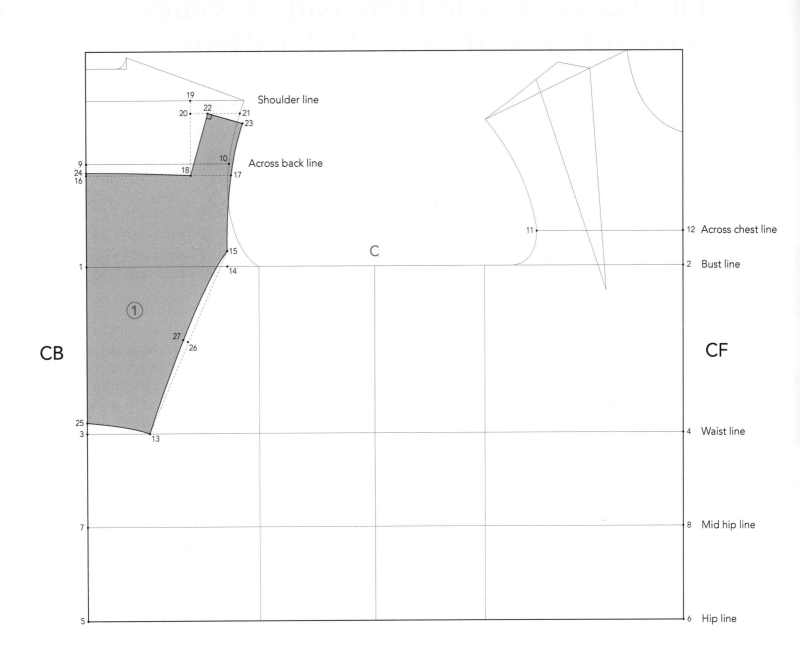

Shoulder line

Across back line

Across chest line — 12

Bust line — 2

CB

CF

Waist line — 4

Mid hip line — 8

Hip line — 6

① 1

C

Plot panel 2 of the 1598 'pair of bodies' onto your traced basic block pattern

Panel 2

4 to **28**	**waist** measurement
2 to **29**	**bust** measurement
28 to **29**	connect with a temporary straight line

Measure temporary line **13** to **15** on **Panel 1** transfer this measurement to **Panel 2** from point **28** through **29** to find point **30**

28 to **31**	half measurement (**28** to **30**)
31 to **32**	square across **0.6cm**

30 through **32** to **28** connect with a concave curve

29 to **33**	one fifth measurement (**2** to **29**) on the **bust** line
33 to **34**	square down **1cm**
12 to **35**	half **across chest** measurement (from your measurement chart) plus **0.5cm**
35 to **36**	square up from point **35** with a temporary line to the **shoulder** line to find point **36**

Note: The position of this temporary line will differ depending on the size of your pattern but should fall within the dart.

35 to **37**	one fifth measurement (**35** to **36**)

37 to **38**	square across **0.5cm** towards the front **armhole** to find point **38**

38 through **35**, **34** to **30** connect with a continuous curve using the basic block front **armhole** as a guide

35 to **39**	one quarter measurement (**12** to **35**) plus **0.5cm**
38 to **40**	square across from point **38** measurement (**22** to **23**) on **Panel 1** to find point **40**
40 to **41**	connect points **40** through **39** with a straight line and extend by **0.5cm** to find point **41**
41 to **12**	connect with a slight convex curve

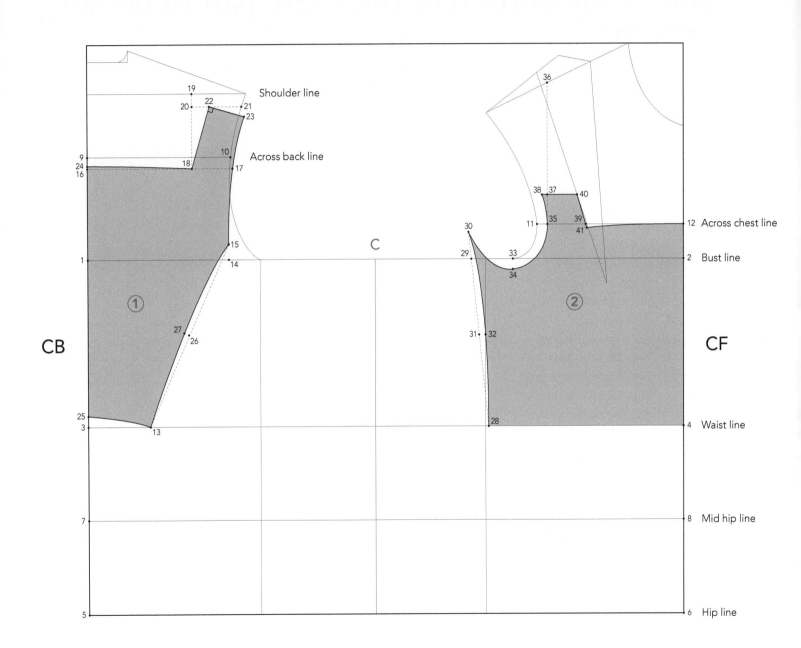

Shoulder line

Across back line

C

CB

CF

Across chest line

Bust line

Waist line

Mid hip line

Hip line

Shape the bottom of the 1598 'pair of bodies' pattern

8 to **42**　　half measurement (**8** to **6**) on **CF** line

4 to **43**　　one third measurement (**4** to **28**)

8 to **44**　　one sixth measurement (**4** to **28**)

42 to **45**　　square across with a temporary line half measurement (**8** to **44**)

45 to **46**　　square up **1cm**

28 to **47**　　one third measurement (**4** to **28**) minus **1cm**

43 to **48**　　half measurement (**4** to **43**) draw a temporary line at a **45** degree angle to line (**4** to **28**) using the diagram as a guide

28 through **47**, **48**, **44** to **46** connect with a deep concave curve

46 to **42**　　connect with a slight concave curve

47 to **49**　　one quarter measurement (**47** to **48**) this marks the location of the front tab

Shoulder line

Across back line

Across chest line

Bust line

C

CB

CF

Waist line

Mid hip line

Hip line

Plot the tabs for the 1598 'pair of bodies'

The size of the tabs will be determined by the length of your corset along the **waist**line, for larger sizes the number of tabs may increase. The back **panel 1** has one tab on each side, however larger sizes may want to increase this to two tabs; this is optional. The front **panel 2** has two tabs on each side, again larger sizes may want to increase this to three tabs. The number of tabs is an aesthetic decision that could be made at the fitting stage.

Panel 1 back tab/tabs

1 to **2** measurement (**25** to **13**) on **panel 1** connect with a straight line

Alternatively for two tabs

1 to **2** half measurement (**25** to **13**) on **panel 1** connect with a straight line
1 to **3** half measurement (**1** to **2**)
3 to **4** square down with a temporary line **5cm**
5 to **6** measurement (**1** to **2**) plus **1.4cm** distribute equally either side of point **4** connect with a straight line
1 to **5** connect with a straight line
2 to **6** connect with a straight line

Round off the corners at points **5** and **6**

Panel 2 front tabs

7 to **8** half measurement (**28** to **49**) on **panel 2** connect with a straight line

Alternatively for three tabs

7 to **8** one third measurement (**28** to **49**) on **panel 2** connect with a straight line
7 to **9** half measurement (**7** to **8**)
9 to **10** square down with a temporary line **5cm**
11 to **12** measurement (**7** to **8**) plus **1.4cm** distribute equally either side of point **10** connect with a straight line
7 to **11** connect with a straight line
8 to **12** connect with a straight line

Round off the corners at points **11** and **12**

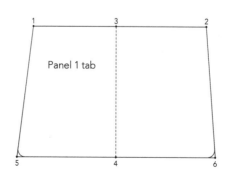

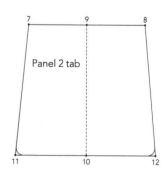

Plot the 1598 'pair of bodies' shoulder strap

A guide to the length of your strap

Take the following measurements from your pattern

Panel 1

point **22** on the **shoulder** line of your corset pattern square up to the back **shoulder** of your traced female basic block pattern

Panel 2

point **37** to point **36** on the front **shoulder** line of your traced female basic block These two measurements added together will give you an approximate length for your strap

1 to **2**   strap length (calculated from your pattern) plus **2cm**

1 to **3**	square up the length of the **shoulder** (**22** to **23**) **panel 1** with a temporary line
3 to **4**	square across **2cm**
4 to **1**	connect with a straight line
2 to **5**	square up measurement (**1** to **3**) on your strap
4 to **5**	connect with a straight line

Ensure that line (**1** to **4**) is the same length as your **shoulder** (**22** to **23**) **panel 1** and that line (**2** to **5**) is the same length as your **shoulder** (**38** to **40**) **panel 3** – adjust if necessary

The strap will connect to the corset at the following points

1 to **4**	will connect to **22** to **23**
2 to **5**	will connect to **38** to **40**

Draw the bone channels on your completed 1598 'pair of bodies' pattern

The 1598 pair of bodies pattern has a wide centre bone and the remaining bones on the front panel are shaped around the bust. The number of bones you wish to use will differ depending on the size of your garment and the rigidity that you require;

you may also opt to fully bone the front to be accurate to the original garment. The shaping around the bust on the front panel can also be omitted. Use the diagram as a guide when drawing the bone channels for your corset. These can

be **1cm** wide or smaller depending on the width of the boning you choose to use; the narrower boning is more historically accurate. The eyelet channel at the centre back is **1.3cm** wide.

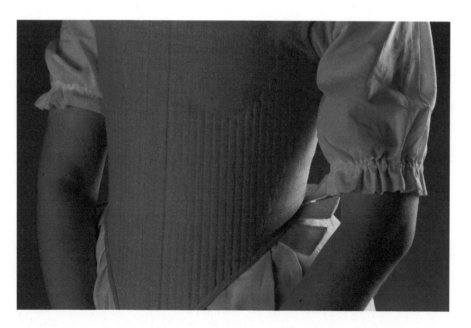

When tracing your pattern it is vital that you note where your panels will join when sewn together. You may want to replace the numbers with a common letter or number to simplify the process of matching these. The tabs are sewn onto the corset along the **waist**line once it is completed.

Panel 1 points **15** to **13** will be sewn to **Panel 2** points **30** to **28**

Panel 1 points **22** to **23** will join to **strap** points **1** to **4**

Panel 2 points **38** to **40** will join to **strap** points **2** to **5**

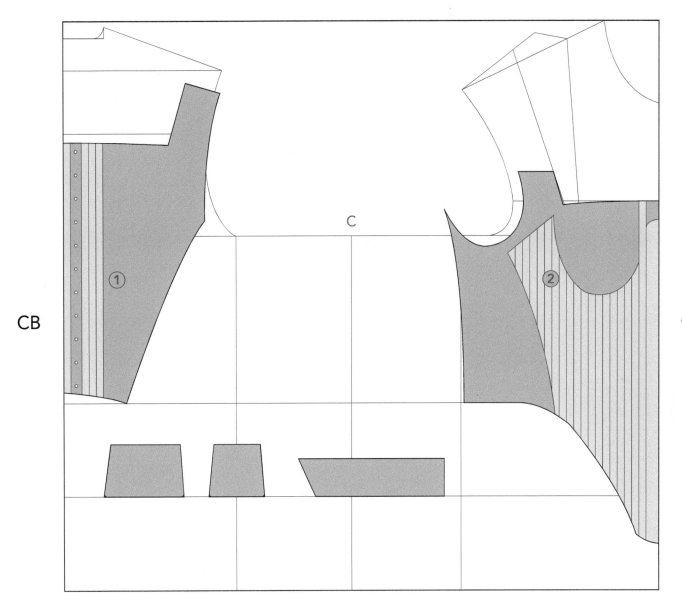

CB

C

CF

8 1680–1700 cream silk
fully-boned corset bodice

1680–1700 cream silk fully-boned corset bodice

The corset bodice held at the Russell Cotes Art Gallery and Museum in Bournemouth, is extremely rare and the exact date is not known although it is thought to be between 1680 and 1700. There is a small label that accompanies the corset that has the name Mrs. J.W. Jackson and an address in Wimborne, Dorset. With this is a small piece of the original lace that tied the shoulder strap to the front. Very few garments from this period have survived and although the cream silk has deteriorated in places the gold and silver raised gilt embroidery is in extremely good condition. Some panels of the corset have been conserved by sewing a silk organza over them to prevent further deterioration of the original fabric. The corset bodice is fully lined in a plain chartreuse yellow silk; this also appears to be part of the conservation work on the bodice.

Opposite: Front view of the 1680–1700 cream silk corset bodice.

Image courtesy of the Russell Cotes Art Gallery and Museum, Bournemouth, England. Photograph by Roger Allen.

Examining this corset has been extremely difficult as the work done to protect the garment has meant that most of the layers under the lining are hidden. It has also been mounted onto a separate linen foundation specifically made to support the garment whilst it is displayed. What I have been able to establish is that the corset is fully boned, hand stitched throughout and is made from layers of linen and silk. It is extremely stiff and heavy. The linen canvas base layers appear to be made up of five panels plus straps, two back and two side panels and a wide and long front panel. The silk top fabric has been sewn onto the boned foundation layers of the corset. These outer layers at the front and sides do not align with the boned foundation, but are decorated and shaped to enhance the wearer's figure and give the illusion of a small waist. The tabs are covered independently to each bodice panel in the same cream silk.

The front and back of the corset are long and pointed, the centre front is 40cm (15.75 inches) long and the centre back is 52cm (20.5 inches) long. The back is particularly rigid, with a thicker piece of whalebone that is the full length of the corset. The eyelets at the centre back are on a panel that sits under the finished edge so they were hidden when the bodice was laced. The corset has a bust measurement of 86cm (34 inches) and a waist measurement of 70cm (27.5 inches). The back panel is long with a deep curve and narrow base, the shoulder straps are angled to go across the top of the arm and are tied at the front. The corset bodice has a total of thirty tabs, fifteen on each side, that are particularly long and thin, the longest being 12.5cm (5 inches) long.

This corset bodice is slightly more challenging than later versions, however it is worth the effort as the final result produces a very attractive 17th-century silhouette. To simplify the pattern I have reduced the number of tabs from fifteen on each side to twelve. This is still enough to give the garment an authentic period feel. The number of bones in each panel are also reduced to ease the construction process and the overall cost. These are 0.5cm wide to match those in the corset, although wider bones can be used.

Original 1680–1700 cream silk fully-boned corset bodice pattern

The lines on the 1680–1700 historical corset bodice pattern diagram opposite are a guide for drafting the new pattern onto the female basic block. The approximate position of the **bust** line and **waist**line are shown on the diagram; it is also labelled with the **CB** and **CF** and line **C** which is an additional guideline for the position of **Panel 2**.

Front and back views of the original 1680–1700 corset bodice showing the seam lines of the applied cream silk.

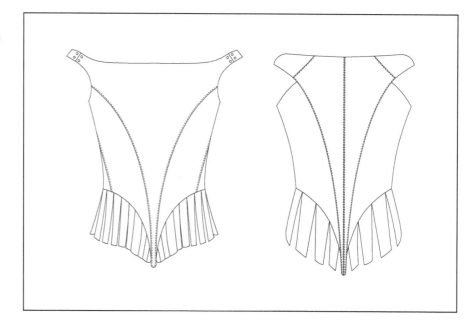

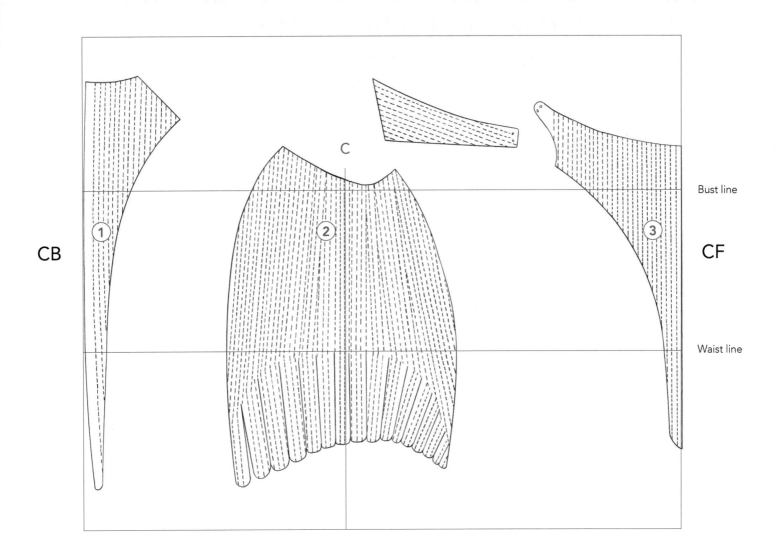

CB

CF

C

Bust line

Waist line

①

②

③

Guidelines for the 1680–1700 cream silk fully-boned corset bodice pattern

Trace and separate the female basic block pattern following the instructions in Chapter 5, 'Preparing the female basic block for your historic pattern'. Leave a gap of **30cm** between the basic block back side seam and basic block front side seam and number each line.

Draw in the following additional guidelines

7 to **8**   **mid-hip** line

The **mid-hip** line lies half measurement (**3** to **5**) square across from the **CB** line to the **CF** line

9 to **10**   **lower mid-hip** line

The **lower mid-hip** line lies half measurement (**7** to **5**) square across from the **CB** line to the **CF** line

11 to **12**   **across back** line
13 to **14**   **across chest** line

Back detail of the 1680–1700 Cream Silk Corset Bodice, showing the wide neckline and long centre back.

Image courtesy of the Russell Cotes Art Gallery and Museum, Bournemouth, England. Photograph by Roger Allen.

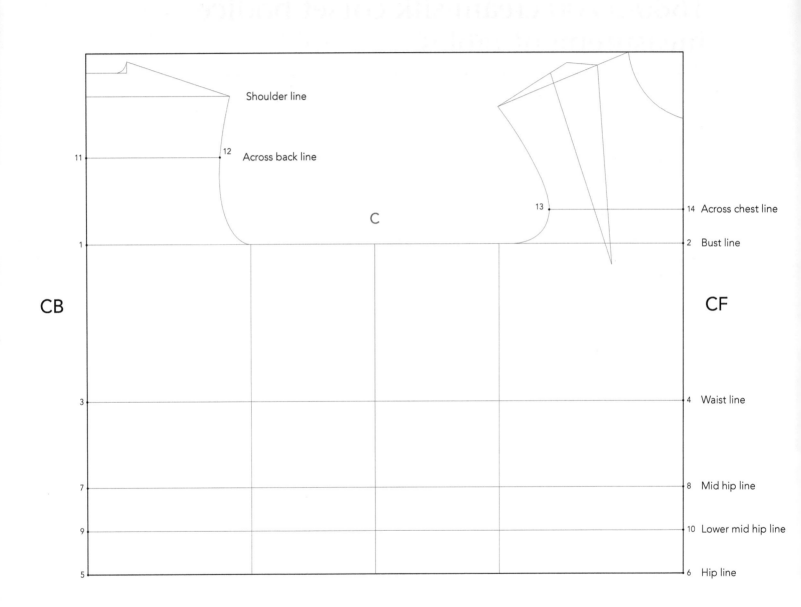

Shoulder line

11 •———————————•12 Across back line

C

13 •———————• 14 Across chest line

1 •———————————• 2 Bust line

CB   CF

3 •———————————• 4 Waist line

7 •———————————• 8 Mid hip line

9 •———————————• 10 Lower mid hip line

5 •———————————• 6 Hip line

1680–1700 cream silk corset bodice measurement tables

The tables below contain measurements for each pattern piece. Find the **bust** and **waist** measurements that relate to your model. The calculation for the size of each panel is recorded horizontally to these measurements.

1680–1700 corset bodice measurement table for the bust

Bust measurement	Reduced bust measurement	Half reduced bust measurement	Panel 1	Panel 2	Panel 3
80cm	78cm	39cm	5.2cm	18.2cm	15.6cm
82cm	80cm	40cm	5.3cm	18.7cm	16cm
86cm	84cm	42cm	5.6cm	19.6cm	16.8cm
90cm	88cm	44cm	5.9cm	20.5cm	17.6cm
94cm	92cm	46cm	6.1cm	21.5cm	18.4cm
100cm	98cm	49cm	6.5cm	22.9cm	19.6cm
106cm	104cm	52cm	6.9cm	24.3cm	20.8cm
112cm	110cm	55cm	7.3cm	25.7cm	22cm
118cm	116cm	58cm	7.7cm	27.1cm	23.2cm
124cm	122cm	61cm	8.1cm	28.5cm	24.4cm

1680–1700 corset bodice measurement table for the waist

Full waist measurement	Reduced waist measurement	Half reduced waist measurement	Panel 1	Panel 2	Panel 3
62cm	57cm	28.5cm	1.6cm	24.5cm	2.4cm
64cm	59cm	29.5cm	1.7cm	25.3cm	2.5cm
68cm	63cm	31.5cm	1.8cm	27cm	2.7cm
72cm	67cm	33.5cm	1.9cm	28.7cm	2.9cm
76cm	71cm	35.5cm	2cm	30.4cm	3.1cm
82cm	77cm	38.5cm	2.2cm	33cm	3.3cm
88cm	83cm	41.5cm	2.4cm	35.6cm	3.5cm
94cm	89cm	44.5cm	2.6cm	38.1cm	3.8cm
100cm	95cm	47.5cm	2.7cm	40.7cm	4.1cm
104cm	99cm	49.5cm	2.8cm	42.5cm	4.2cm

Create a table of measurements for your model

Create an individual table for your model
to isolate the specific measurements
required to draft your historical pattern.
See example table below.

1680–1700 corset bodice individual measurement table example

Size	Full measurement	Reduced measurement	Half reduced measurement	Panel 1	Panel 2	Panel 3
Bust	90cm	88cm	44cm	5.9cm	20.5cm	17.6cm
Waist	68cm	63cm	31.5cm	1.8cm	27cm	2.7cm

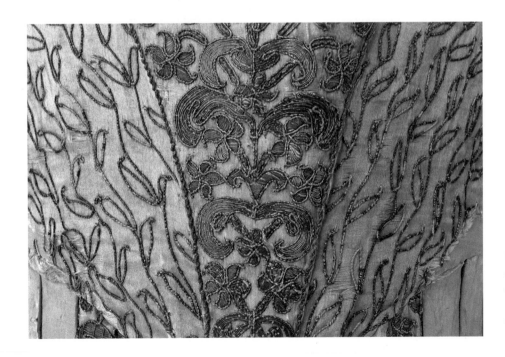

Detail of the raised silver and gold gilt
embroidery that decorates the front panel
of the 1680 –1700 cream silk corset bodice.

Image courtesy of the Russell Cotes Art
Gallery and Museum, Bournemouth,
England. Photograph by Roger Allen.

Begin plotting the 1680–1700 cream silk corset bodice onto your traced basic block pattern

Panel 1

3 to **15**	**waist** measurement
1 to **16**	**bust** measurement
16 to **15**	connect with a temporary straight line

Panel 3

4 to **17**	**waist** measurement
2 to **18**	**bust** measurement minus **0.5cm**
18 to **19**	square up **1cm**
19 to **17**	connect with a temporary straight line

Note: The overall position of **Panel 3** will differ slightly depending on the size of your corset.

Panel 2

20 to **21**	**waist** measurement distribute evenly either side of line **C**
22 to **23**	**bust** measurement distribute three fifths to the left of line **C** and two fifths to the right of line **C**
22 to **20**	connect with a temporary straight line
23 to **21**	connect with a temporary straight line

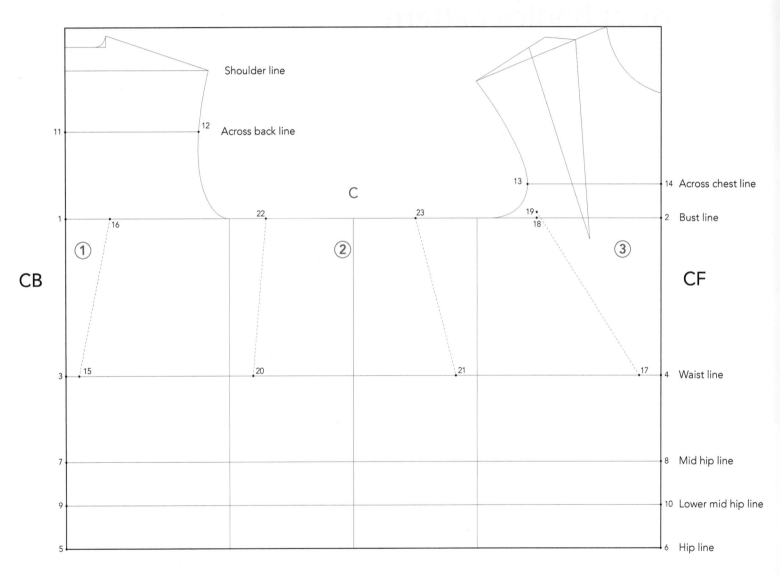

Shoulder line

Across back line

Across chest line

C

Bust line

CB

CF

Waist line

Mid hip line

Lower mid hip line

Hip line

Extend the top of the 1680–1700 cream silk corset bodice pattern

Panel 1

24	lies at the junction of the **CB** line and the **shoulder** line
11 to **25**	two fifths measurement (**11** to **12**) on the **across back** line
25 to **26**	square up from point **25** with a temporary line to the **shoulder** line to find point **26**
24 to **27**	one third (**11** to **24**) on **CB** line
27 to **28**	square across from point **27** to temporary line (**25** to **26**) to find point **28**
28 to **29**	**1cm** on line (**25** to **26**)
27 to **29**	connect with a shallow concave curve
12 to **30**	one fifth (**11** to **12**) on **across back** line

29 to **30**	connect with a straight line
16 to **30**	connect with a temporary straight line

The angle of your **shoulder** may differ slightly from the diagram and will depend on the proportion and size of your model

16 to **31**	half measurement (**16** to **30**)
31 to **32**	square across **1.3cm**

30 through **32** and **16** to **15** connect with a continuous concave curve using the diagram as a guide

Extend the **across back** line (**11** to **12**) to level with point **23** on **Panel 2**, this will be used later to position the top of **Panel 2**

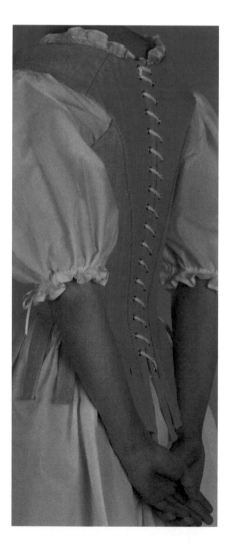

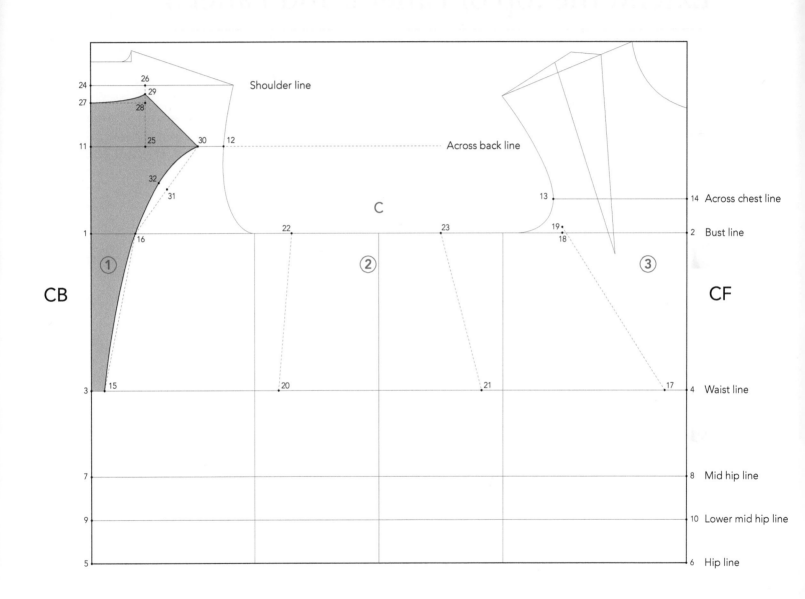

Shoulder line

Across back line

Across chest line — 14

C

Bust line — 2

① ② ③

CB CF

Waist line — 4

Mid hip line — 8

Lower mid hip line — 10

Hip line — 6

Extend the top of Panel 2 and Panel 3

Panel 2

22 to 33   one tenth measurement
(**22** to **23**) plus **1cm**

33 to 34   square up from point **33** with
a temporary line to extended
across back line to find point
34

34 to 35   one fifth measurement
(**33** to **34**) plus **1cm**

23 to 36   one tenth measurement
(**22** to **23**)

36 to 37   square up from point **36** with
a temporary line to extended
across back line to find
point **37**

36 to 38   one fifth measurement
(**36** to **37**)

39   lies at the junction of the **bust**
line and line **C**

39 to 39a   square up **1cm**

35 through **39a** to **38** connect with a deep
concave curve using the diagram as a
guide

20 to 40   half measurement (**20** to **22**)
40 to 41   square across **1.2cm**

21 to 42   half measurement (**21** to **23**)
42 to 43   square across **1.4cm**
35 to 22   connect with a very slight
convex curve
38 to 23   connect with a very slight
convex curve

Panel 3

14 to 44 **1cm** on **CF** line

13 to 45 square up from point **13** with
a temporary line measurement
(**2** to **14**) found on the **CF** to
find point **45**

45 to 46 **2cm** at a **45** degree angle from
line (**13** to **45**)

46 to 19 connect with a temporary
straight line

19 to 47 half measurement (**19** to **46**)

47 to 48 square across **0.7cm**

46 through **48** to **19** connect with a
concave curve

45 to **44** connect with a shallow concave
curve (this should be at a **90**
degree angle to line **45** to **46**
at point **45**)

17 to **49** half measurement (**17** to **19**)
49 to **50** square across **1.8cm**
19 through **50** to **17** connect with a
concave curve

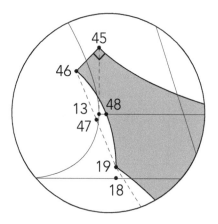

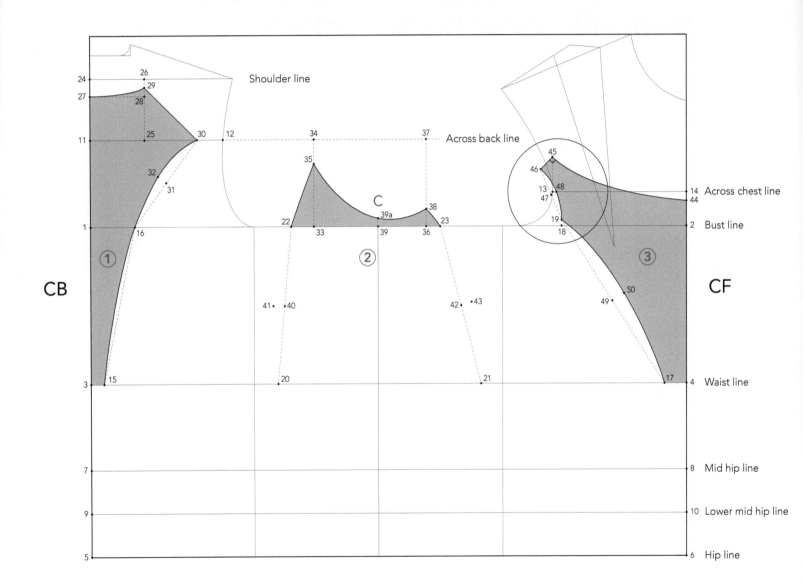

Shoulder line

Across back line

C

Across chest line

Bust line

CB

CF

Waist line

Mid hip line

Lower mid hip line

Hip line

Extend the bottom of the 1680–1700 cream silk corset bodice pattern

Panel 1

9 to **51**	half measurement (**9** to **5**) on the **CB** line
51 to **52**	square across half **waist** measurement (**3** to **15**)
15 to **52**	extend line (**30** through **32** and **16** to **15**) to point **52**
52 to **51**	connect with a curve at point **52**

Panel 3

10 to **53**	one fifth measurement (**8** to **10**) on **CF** line
53 to **54**	square across from point **53** half **waist** measurement (**4** to **17**) to find point **54**

Extend line **19** through **50** and **17** to **54** with a continuous concave curve using the diagram as a guide

54 to **10**	connect with a convex curve

Panel 2

20 to **55**	square down from point **20** with a temporary line to the **hip** line to find point **55**
55 to **56**	**2.5cm** on the hip line

22 through **41** to **56** connect with a continuous convex curve
Note: this line may not go through point **20**

57	lies at the junction of the **waist**line and line **C**
58	lies at the junction of the **mid hip** line and line **C**
58 to **59**	**2cm**
56 to **60**	three fifths measurement (**9** to **5**) on **CB** line
21 to **61**	square down from point **21** with a temporary line to the **lower mid-hip** line to find point **61**
61 to **62**	**1cm** on **lower mid-hip** line

23 through **43**, **21** and **64** to **62** connect with a smooth continuous convex curve

60 to **59**	connect with a temporary straight line
59 to **62**	connect with a temporary straight line

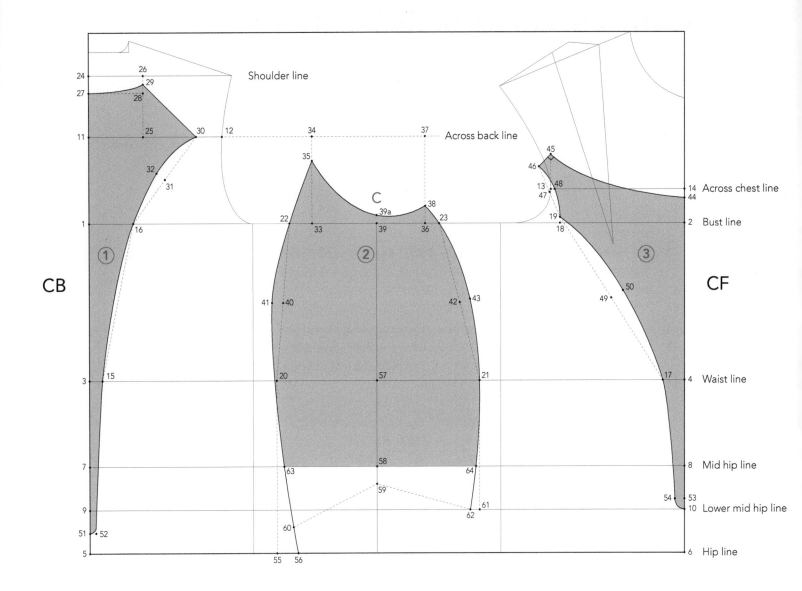

Shoulder line

Across back line

Across chest line

Bust line

Waist line

Mid hip line

Lower mid hip line

Hip line

CB

CF

C

① ② ③

Extend the bottom of the 1680–1700 cream silk corset bodice pattern

Panel 2 continued

63 lies at the junction of line (**22** through **41** to **60**) and the **mid hip** line

63 to **57**   connect with a temporary straight line

64   lies at the junction of line (**23** through **43** and **21** to **62**) and the **mid hip** line

64 to **57**   connect with a temporary straight line

57 to **65**   one third measurement (**57** to **63**)

65 to **66**   square up from point **65** with a temporary line to the **waist**line to find point **66**

66 to **67**   **2cm** on line (**65** to **66**)

57 through **67** to **63** connect with a deep convex curve using the diagram as a guide

57 to **68**   half measurement (**57** to **64**)

68 to **69**   square up from point **68** with a temporary line to the **waist**line to find point **69**

68 to **70**   half measurement (**68** to **69**) minus **0.5cm**

57 through **70** to **64** connect with a deep convex curve using the diagram as a guide

Note: whilst creating the curve of the **waist**line leave the arc either side of point **57** straight for approximately **5cm**, **2.5cm** either side of point **57**; this may be longer for larger sizes

59 to **71**   one third measurement (**59** to **60**)

71 to **72**   square up **0.5cm**

59 to **73**   half measurement (**59** to **62**)

73 to **74**   square up **1cm**

60 through **72**, **59** and **74** to **62** connect with a concave curve using the diagram as a guide

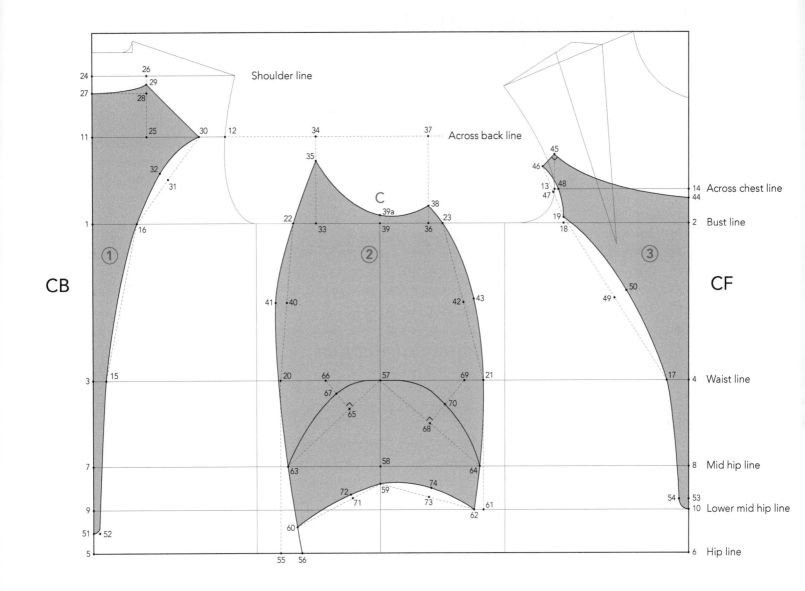

Shoulder line

Across back line

C

Across chest line

Bust line

CB

CF

①

②

③

Waist line

Mid hip line

Lower mid hip line

Hip line

Plot the tabs for the 1680–1700 cream silk corset bodice pattern

Note: The exact position of the tabs will differ depending on the size and proportion of your model

57 to **75**	3cm
57 to **76**	3cm
64 to **77**	3cm
62 to **78**	3cm
77 to **78**	connect with a straight line
63 to **79**	3cm
79 to **80**	draw in an even width tab from point **79** mirroring line (**63** to **60**) down to find point **80**

Top edge of tabs

Measure line **79** through **67** to **75** divide by **4** to find points **81, 82** and **83** – point **83** may fall close to point **67**

Bottom edge of tabs

Measure line **80** through **72** to **59** divide by **5** to find points **84, 85, 86** and **87** – point **86** may fall close to point **72**

81 to **84**	connect with a straight line
82 to **85**	connect with a straight line
83 to **86**	connect with a straight line
75 to **87**	connect with a straight line

Top edge of tabs

Measure line **76** through **70** to **77** divide by **4** to find points **88, 89** and **90** – point **89** may fall close to point **70**

Bottom edge of tabs

Measure line **59** through **74** to **78** divide by **5** to find points **91, 92, 93** and **94**

76 to **91**	connect with a straight line
88 to **92**	connect with a straight line
89 to **93**	connect with a straight line
90 to **94**	connect with a straight line

Additional guide points for joining the corset

Panel 1

52 to **95** is the same as tab measurement (**60** to **63**) **Panel 2** plus **2.5cm**

Measure line **35** through **22** and **41** to **63** on **Panel 2** transfer measurement to **Panel 1** from point **95** through **15, 16** and **32** to find point **96**

Panel 3

Measure line **38** through **23, 43** and **21** to **64** on **Panel 2** transfer measurement to **Panel 3** from point **19** through **50** and **17** to find point **97**.

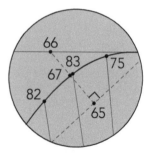

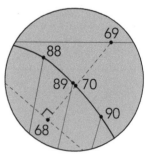

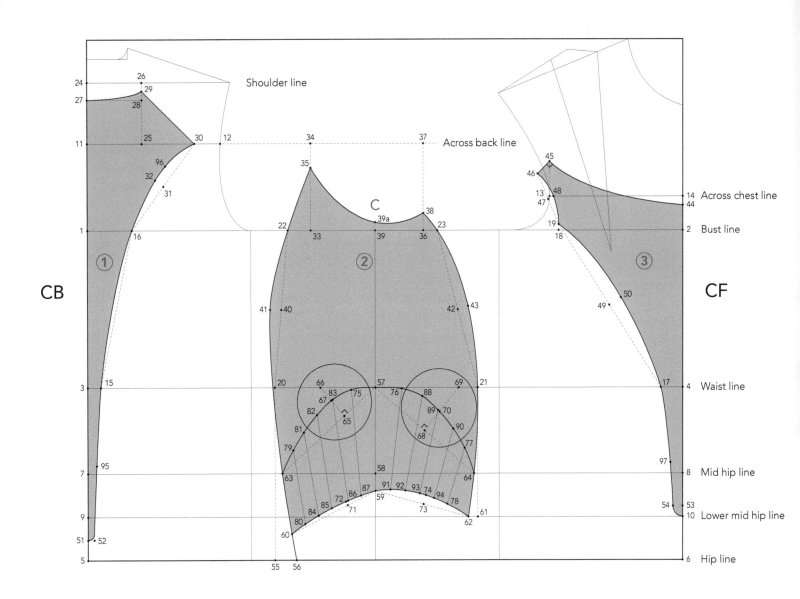

CB

CF

Shoulder line

Across back line

Across chest line

Bust line

Waist line

Mid hip line

Lower mid hip line

Hip line

C

① ② ③

Plot the 1680–1700 cream silk corset bodice shoulder strap pattern

A guide to the length of your strap

Take the following measurements from your pattern

Panel 1

Point **30** on the **shoulder** line of your stays pattern to the back **shoulder** of your traced female basic block pattern

Panel 3

Point **45** on the front of your corset pattern to the front **shoulder** of your traced female basic block pattern

These two measurements added together will give you an approximate strap length

1 to 2 strap length (as calculated from your pattern) plus **3cm**

1 to 3 square up the **shoulder** measurement **Panel 1** (**29** to **30**) minus **0.5cm**

3 to 4 square across **2.5cm** from point **3** to find point **4**

4 to 1 connect with a straight line

Ensure that the strap measurement (**4** to **1**) is the same length as the **shoulder** measurement of your stays pattern (**29**

to **30**) **Panel 1**, adjust if necessary. This is where the strap will connect to the back of the bodice when constructed

2 to 5 square up **2cm**

4 to 5 connect with a concave curve using the diagram as a guide

Round off the corners of the strap at points **5** and **2**

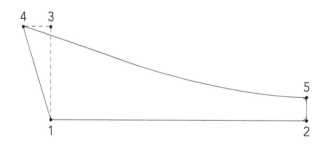

Draw the bone channels on your completed 1680–1700 corset bodice pattern

The number of bones differs from the original corset bodice which is fully boned, this is optional and will depend on the final finish you require. Use the diagram provided as a guide and amend the number of bones depending on the size of your corset bodice and the rigidity that you require. The bone channels in this pattern are **0.7cm** wide to fit a bone that is **0.5cm** wide; this is close to the original garment and suits the style and period of the corset bodice. The centre back of **Panel 1** is laced. This is extremely slim and may only allow you enough room for eyelets at the very centre back. Metal bones with eyelet holes for the centre back opening are available and could be a good solution for this particular corset bodice. If these are not available the other option is to place a bone down the centre back and eyelet to the side of the bone; there is enough room to eyelet to just below the waist.

When tracing your pattern it is vital that you note where your panels will join when sewn together. You may want to replace the numbers with a common letter to simplify the process of matching these. The tabs are left open to spread over the hips.

Panel 1 points (**96** to **95**) will be sewn to **Panel 2** points (**35** to **63**)

Panel 2 points (**38** to **64**) will be sewn to **Panel 3** points (**19** to **97**)

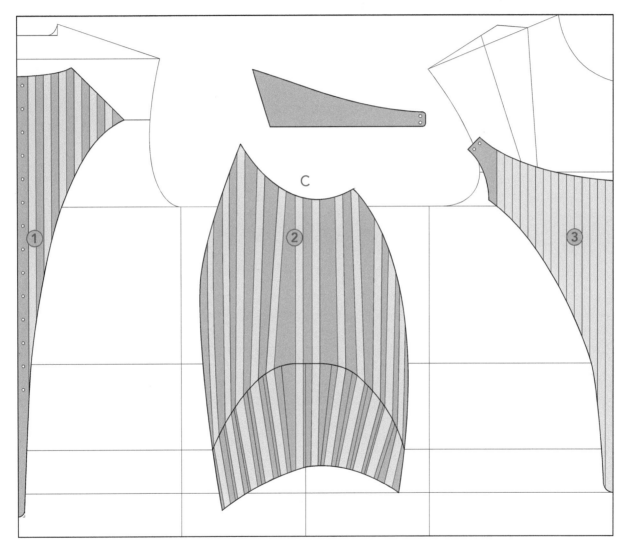

CB

CF

C

9 1760 silk brocade corset bodice

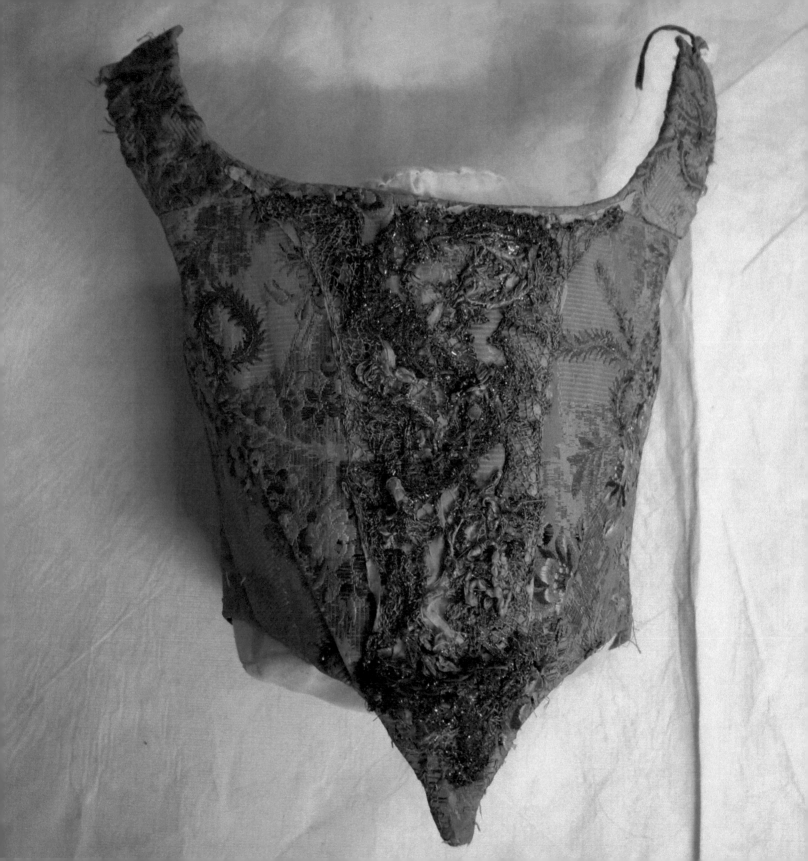

1760 silk brocade corset bodice

This corset bodice is part of the Charles Paget Wade collection held at Berrington Hall, Herefordshire and is thought to date around 1760, although the exact date is not known. It is made from a beautiful orchid pink French silk brocade with a floral design and is decorated with chenille, metal thread and fly braid at the centre front that creates the effect of a stomacher. The bodice has six pieces: two back panels, two side panels and two front panels. The straps are part of the front panel. The centre front has a very deep shallow point; there is a seam but this is only visible on the linen backing fabric as the front top fabric decoration covers this.

The centre back has six eyelet holes on one side and seven on the other. The corset bodice has no tabs around the waist and the straps are sewn to the front and left open and tied at the back so as not to be visible; these were tied with a thin blue ribbon. The bodice has been enlarged, possibly when the back linen panels were sewn to the front; it appears that the same fabric has been used at different times on the bodice as the amount of wear and fading is not consistent.

The bodice at Berrington Hall is extremely small: it has a 64cm (25.25 inches) bust and 34cm (13.5 inches) waist, the centre back is 27cm (10.5 inches) long and the centre front is 29cm (11.5 inches) long. The sizing suggests that it may have belonged to a young girl of approximately twelve years old. The bodice has a plain light brown linen back so was not made to be seen; the beautiful front indicates that it may have been worn with a sack gown.

The bodice is fully-boned with additional horizontal shaping bones across the front. It is laced at the centre back. The bones are 1cm, wider than those used on a typical woman's bodice during this period, again supporting the possible age of the wearer.

This pattern is relatively straightforward as it has no tabs and only three main pattern pieces. The original corset bodice has forty two bones in each half; I have reduced the number of bones in this corset to ease the construction process, comfort of the wearer and cost. The bone channels are placed in the appropriate position to give support and structure to the corset, and to create an accurate historical silhouette. I have lowered the neckline to suit a woman's figure, as the original was for a younger wearer.

Opposite: Front view of the 1760 silk brocade corset bodice. Part of the Charles Paget Wade collection, Snowshill Manor, held by the National Trust at Berrington Hall, Herefordshire, England.

Reproduced by kind permission of the National Trust.

Original 1760 silk brocade corset bodice pattern

The lines on the 1760 historical stays pattern diagram opposite are a guide for drafting the new pattern onto the female basic block. The approximate position of the **bust** line and **waist**line are shown on the diagram, it is also labelled with the **CB** and **CF** and line **C** which is an additional guideline for the position of **Panel 2**.

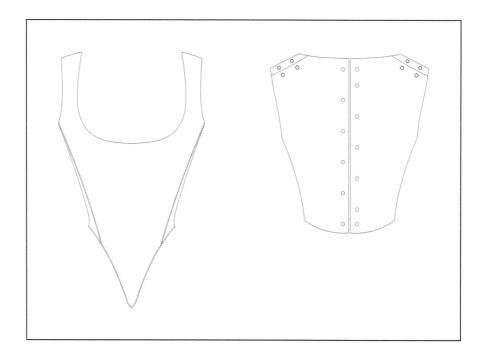

Opposite: 1760 corset bodice pattern diagram showing additional guidelines for the placement of the stays on the basic block pattern.

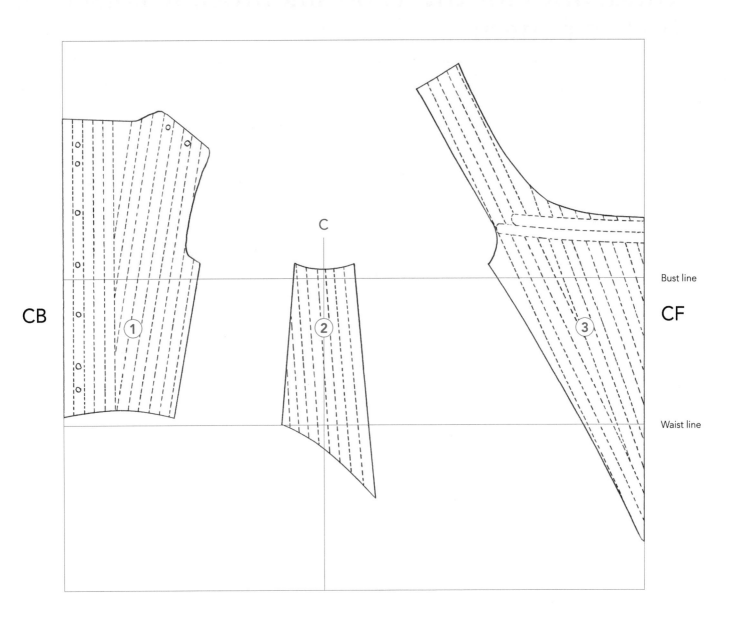

CB

C

CF

Bust line

Waist line

①

②

③

Guidelines for the 1760 silk brocade corset bodice pattern

Trace and separate the female basic block pattern following the instructions in Chapter 5, 'Preparing the female basic block for your historic pattern'. Leave a gap of **25cm** between the basic block back side seam and basic block front side seam and number each line.

Draw in the following additional guidelines

7 to **8**   **mid-hip** line

The **mid-hip** line lies half measurement (**3** to **5**) square across from the **CB** line to the **CF** line

9 to **10**   **across chest** line

Front detail of the 1760 corset bodice revealing the beautiful chenille decoration applied to the front of the corset bodice.

Reproduced by kind permission of the National Trust

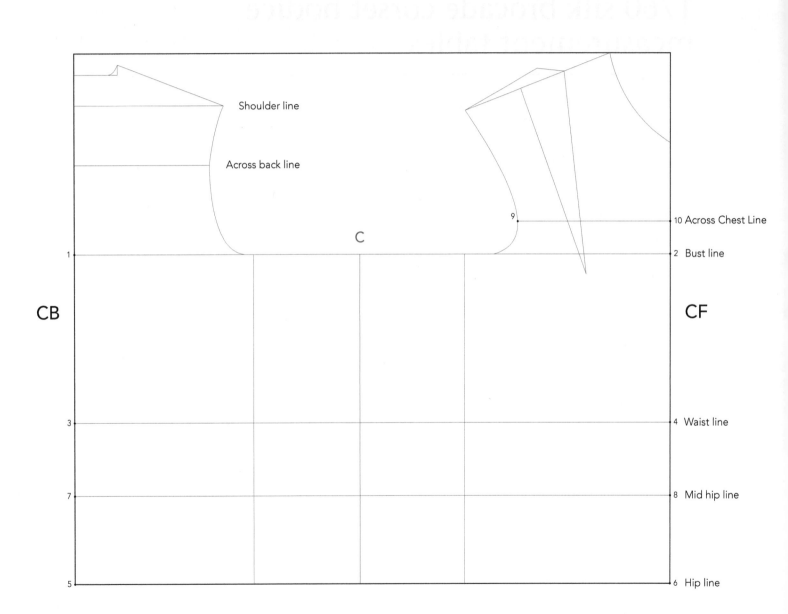

Shoulder line

Across back line

C

1   9   10 Across Chest Line

2   Bust line

CB   CF

3   4   Waist line

7   8   Mid hip line

5   6   Hip line

1760 silk brocade corset bodice measurement tables

The tables below contain measurements for each pattern piece. Find the **bust** and **waist** measurements that are the closest to that of your model. The calculation for the size of each panel is recorded horizontally to these measurements.

1760 corset bodice measurement table for the bust

Full bust measurement	Reduced bust measurement	Half reduced bust measurement	Panel 1	Panel 2	Panel 3
80cm	78cm	39cm	15.1cm	6.2cm	17.7cm
82cm	80cm	40cm	15.5cm	6.4cm	18.1cm
86cm	84cm	42cm	16.3cm	6.7cm	19cm
90cm	88cm	44cm	17cm	7cm	20cm
94cm	92cm	46cm	17.8cm	7.3cm	20.9cm
100cm	98cm	49cm	19cm	7.8cm	22.2cm
106cm	104cm	52cm	20.1cm	8.3cm	23.6cm
112cm	110cm	55cm	21.3cm	8.7cm	25cm
118cm	116cm	58cm	22.5cm	9.2cm	26.3cm
124cm	122cm	61cm	23.6cm	9.7cm	27.7cm

1760 corset bodice measurement table for the waist

Full waist measurement	Reduced waist measurement	Half reduced waist measurement	Panel 1	Panel 2	Panel 3
62cm	57cm	28.5cm	12.6cm	8.8cm	7.1cm
64cm	59cm	29.5cm	13cm	9.1cm	7.4cm
68cm	63cm	31.5cm	14cm	9.7cm	7.8cm
72cm	67cm	33.5cm	14.8cm	10.4cm	8.3cm
76cm	71cm	35.5cm	15.7cm	11cm	8.8cm
82cm	77cm	38.5cm	17cm	11.9cm	9.6cm
88cm	83cm	41.5cm	18.4cm	12.8cm	10.3cm
94cm	89cm	44.5cm	19.7cm	13.7cm	11.1cm
100cm	95cm	47.5cm	21cm	14.7cm	11.8cm
104cm	99cm	49.5cm	21.9cm	15.3cm	12.3cm

Create a table of measurements for your model

Create an individual table for your model
to isolate the specific measurements
required to draft your historical pattern.
See example table below.

1760 corset bodice individual measurement table example

Size	Full measurement	Reduced measurement	Half reduced measurement	Panel 1	Panel 2	Panel 3
Bust	80cm	78cm	39cm	15.1cm	6.2cm	17.7cm
Waist	64cm	59cm	29.5cm	13cm	9.1cm	7.3cm

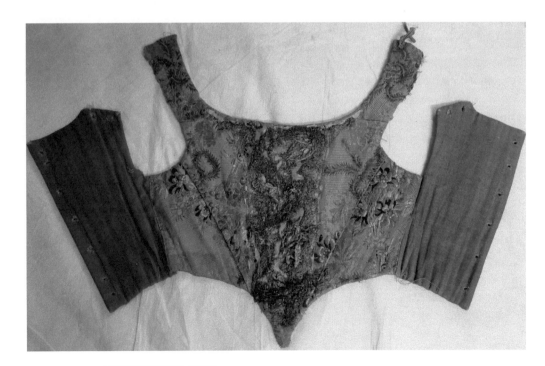

The 1760 Corset bodice
showing the front, side and
brown linen back panels.

Reproduced by kind
permission of the National
Trust.

Begin plotting the 1760 silk brocade corset bodice onto your traced basic block pattern

Panel 1

3 to **11**	**waist** measurement
1 to **12**	**bust** measurement
12 to **11**	connect with a straight line

Panel 3

4 to **13**	**waist** measurement
2 to **14**	**bust** measurement
14 to **13**	connect with a temporary straight line

Panel 2

15 to **16**	**waist** measurement distribute equally either side of line **C**
17 to **18**	**bust** measurement distribute equally either side of line **C**
17 to **15**	connect with a straight line
18 to **16**	connect with a straight line

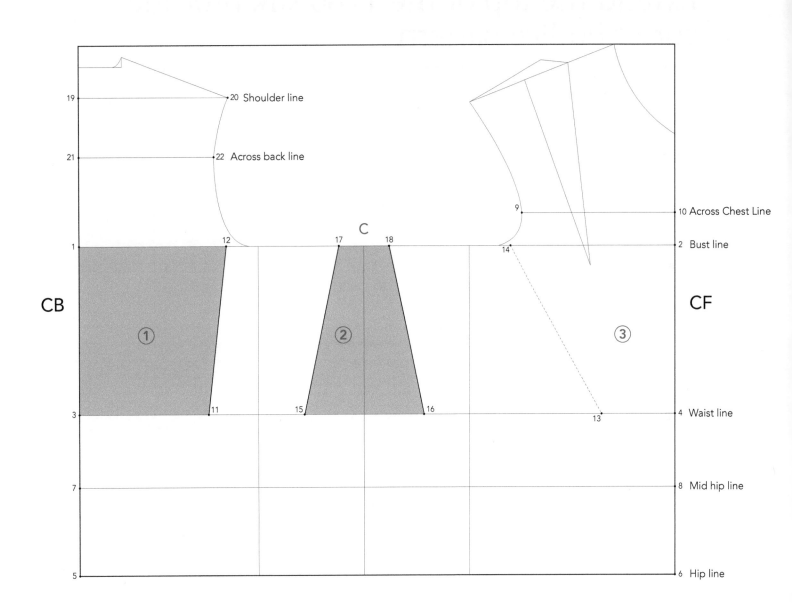

CB

CF

C

19
20 Shoulder line

21
22 Across back line

10 Across Chest Line

9

1
12
17
18
14
2 Bust line

①
②
③

11
15
16
13
4 Waist line

3

7
8 Mid hip line

5
6 Hip line

Extend the top of the 1760 silk brocade corset bodice pattern

Panel 1

19	lies at the junction of the **CB** line and the **shoulder** line
20	lies at the junction of the **shoulder** line and the top of the basic block **armhole**
21	lies at the junction of the **CB** line and the **across back** line
22	lies at the junction of the **across back** line and the basic block **armhole**
19 to **23**	one third measurement (**19** to **21**) on the **CB** line
23 to **24**	square across from point **23** with a temporary line to the traced basic block **armhole** edge to find point **24**
19 to **25**	half measurement (**19** to **20**)
25 to **26**	square up **1cm** from point **25** to find point **26**
19 to **26**	connect with a shallow concave curve

24 to **27**	2.5cm
22 to **28**	2.5cm
26 to **27**	connect with a straight line
12 to **29**	one tenth measurement (**1** to **12**)
29 to **30**	square up **0.7cm**

27 through **28** to **30** connect with a very shallow concave curve

30 to **12**   connect with a very shallow concave curve

Panel 2

17 to **31**	one third measurement (**17** to **18**)
31 to **32**	square down **0.5cm**

17 through **32** to **18** connect with a very shallow concave curve

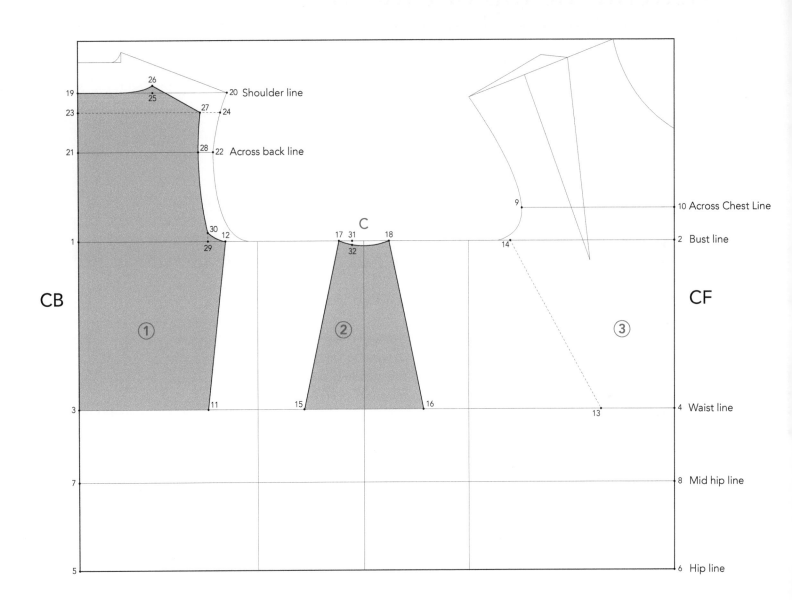

CB

CF

19
23
21

26
25
20 Shoulder line
27 24
28 22 Across back line

C

30
12
29
1

17 31 18
32

9
10 Across Chest Line
14
2 Bust line

① ② ③

11
15 16
3
13
4 Waist line

7
8 Mid hip line

5
6 Hip line

Extend the top of Panel 3

33	lies at the junction of the front **shoulder** line and **armhole** of your basic block
34 and **35**	lie at the junction of the front **shoulder** line and the **bust** dart of your basic block
33 to **36**	half measurement (**34** to **35**) **bust** dart
9 to **37**	1cm
36 to **38**	**shoulder** measurement (**26** to **27**) **Panel 1** minus 0.5cm

14 through **37** to **36** connect with a concave curve using your traced basic block front **armhole** as a guide between points (**14** and **37**). Extend line **2.5cm** beyond point **36** to find point **39**

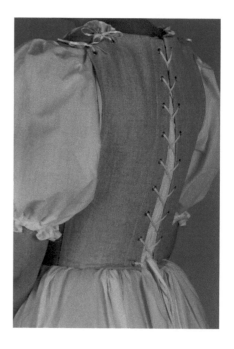

40	lies at the junction of the **bust** dart and the across **chest** line (**9** to **10**)
2 to **41**	one tenth measurement (**2** to **14**)

2 through **41** and **40** to **38** connect with a deep concave curve. Extend line **2cm** beyond point **38** to find point **42**

39 to **42**	connect with a straight line

Ensure that the **shoulder** strap measurement (**39** to **42**) **Panel 3** is the same length as the back **shoulder** measurement of your stays pattern (**26** to **27**) **Panel 1** – adjust if necessary

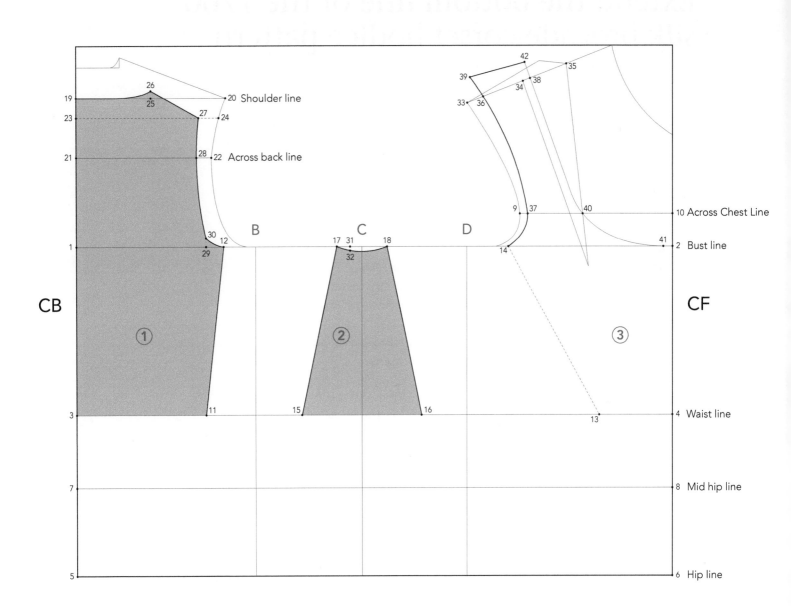

CB

CF

① ② ③

26
25
19
23 27 24
28 22 Across back line
21
20 Shoulder line

B C D
30 12 17 31 18 9 37 40 10 Across Chest Line
1 29 32 14 41 2 Bust line

42
39 35
33 36 34 38

11 15 16 13 4 Waist line
3

7 8 Mid hip line

5 6 Hip line

Extend the bottom line of the 1760 silk brocade corset bodice pattern

Panel 1

3 to **43**	**1cm** on the **CB** line
11 to **43**	connect with a slight concave curve

Panel 2

Ensure that line (**12** to **11**) on **Panel 1** is the same length as (**17** to **15**) on **Panel 2**, extend at point **15** if necessary

16 to **44**	extend line (**18** to **16**) to the **mid-hip** line to find point **44**
44 to **45**	one fifth measurement (**16** to **44**)
15 to **45**	connect with a temporary straight line
45 to **46**	two fifths measurement (**15** to **45**)
46 to **47**	square up **1.5cm**

15 through **47** to **45** connect with a concave curve

Panel 3

8 to **48**	half measurement (**8** to **6**) on **CF** line
48 to **49**	square across **1cm** from point **48** to find point **49**
13 to **49**	connect with a temporary straight line
13 to **50**	half measurement (**13** to **49**)
50 to **51**	square across **0.5cm**

14 through **51** to **49** connect with a very shallow concave curve.

Note: This new line may fall to the left of point **13** by up to **1cm** depending on the size of your pattern

Round off the corner at point **49**

Measure line **18** through **16** to **45** on **Panel 2** transfer this measurement to **Panel 3** from point **14** to find point **52** (this is where the bottom of **Panel 2** will join **Panel 3**)

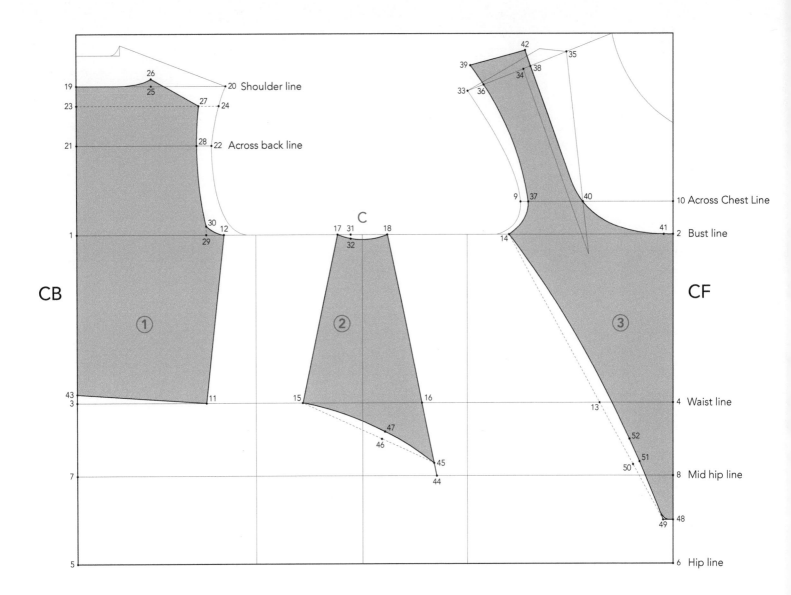

CB

CF

C

26
25
19
20 Shoulder line
23
27
24
21
28 22 Across back line
1
30 12
29
17 31 18
32
9 37
40
10 Across Chest Line
41 2 Bust line
14
42
39
33 36
34 38
35
① ② ③
43
3
11
15
16
13 4 Waist line
47
46
52
51
50
7
45
44
48
49
8 Mid hip line
5
6 Hip line

Draw the bone channels on your completed 1760 silk brocade corset bodice pattern

Use the diagram as a guide to draft your corset bodice bone channels. The number of bones will differ depending on the size of your corset bodice and the rigidity that you require. The bone channels in this pattern are **1cm** wide to fit a bone that is **0.7cm** wide. At the **CB** there are two bone channels with a central eyelet channel that is **1.3cm** wide on both sides for lacing up the stays.

When tracing your pattern it is vital that you number each panel and note where your panels will join when sewn together.

Panel 1 points (**12** to **11**) will be sewn to **Panel 2** points (**17** to **15**)

Panel 2 points (**18** to **45**) will be sewn to **Panel 3** points (**14** to **52**)

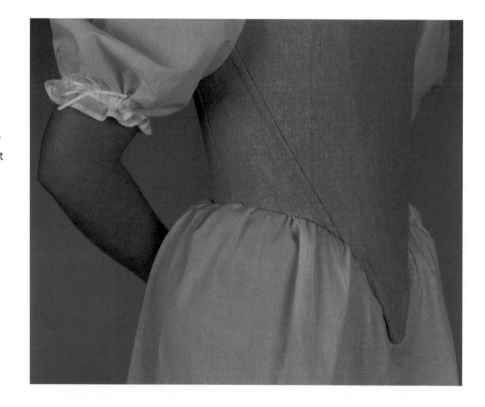

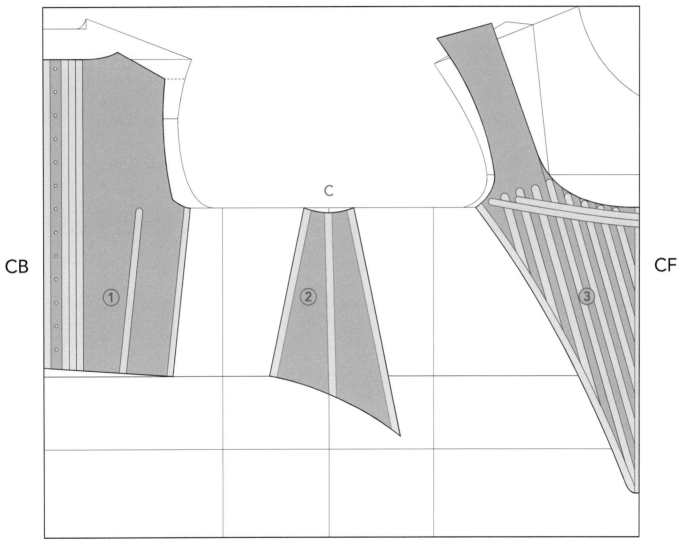

CB

C

CF

① ② ③

10 1760 strapless stays

1760 strapless stays

The stays held at Chilcombe House are part of the Hampshire Cultural Trust collection. They have ten panels and are dated around 1760, there are no straps or the straps have been removed to allow for a wider lower neckline. The stays are made from a beige coloured cotton, lined with natural linen. The fabric layers of the stays are hand stitched together with neat even stitches, creating visible channels where the whalebones of varying widths are placed. The eyelets of the stays are also hand worked and the lace at the centre back is drawn up at a diagonal. The top and bottom edges of the stays are bound with leather. The centre front has a decorative lace that does not appear to be the original.

The stays are fully boned to support its structure, providing the strength to mould the body to the fashionable silhouette of the mid to late 18th century. There are a total of sixteen tabs, eight on each side that are various sizes and shapes.

The lack of beauty and finesse in this garment suggests that it was not a garment that was to be seen by anyone other than the wearer. It has clearly been altered at some point, with an additional panel added to the original, changing it from an eight-panel pair of stays to a ten-panel. This additional panel is not an exact colour match, although they have attempted to replicate the original. It has also been mended and reinforced in various places with either the fabric of the stays or soft leather. There is a large section of darning at the top of the front panel and around the armhole; this could cover previous eyelet holes at the front.

This is a larger garment than many retained by museums, with a 100cm bust (39.5 inches) and a 80cm waist (31 inches); the centre front is 29cm (11.5 inches). The stays have a wide deep neckline and boning that is placed at an angle towards the centre front seam. The tabs on the original are a little uneven; this may be due to the alterations made to the garment so I have adjusted these slightly to improve the overall appearance of the stays. This pattern is particularly good for the fuller figure.

The Hampshire stays pattern is a little more difficult to draft due to the angle of the panels, however the instructions will take you through the drafting process. For smaller sizes I suggest that the two tabs on panel 4 be reduced to one. The size of bone channels and bones have been increased on the final pattern from the original stays width of 0.5cm to 0.7cm. This will accommodate a 0.5cm bone which is more readily available and will still provide an authentic look and shape to the final garment. The lacing at the centre back of the stays has also been amended from the original diagonal lacing, to make lacing the garment less complicated, and I have reduced the number of bones; these changes are optional.

Opposite: 1760 buff strapless stays.
From the collections of Hampshire Cultural Trust.

Original 1760 strapless stays

The lines on the 1760 historical stays pattern diagram opposite are a guide for drafting the new pattern onto the female basic block. The approximate position of the **bust** line and **waist**line are shown on the diagram; it is also labelled with the **CB** and **CF**. Lines **A**, **B**, **C** and **D** are additional guidelines for the position of **Panel 2**, **Panel 3** and **Panel 4**.

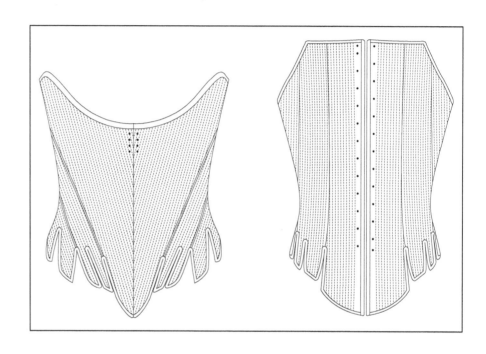

Front and back views of the original 1760 buff strapless stays showing the original stitch lines and bone channels.

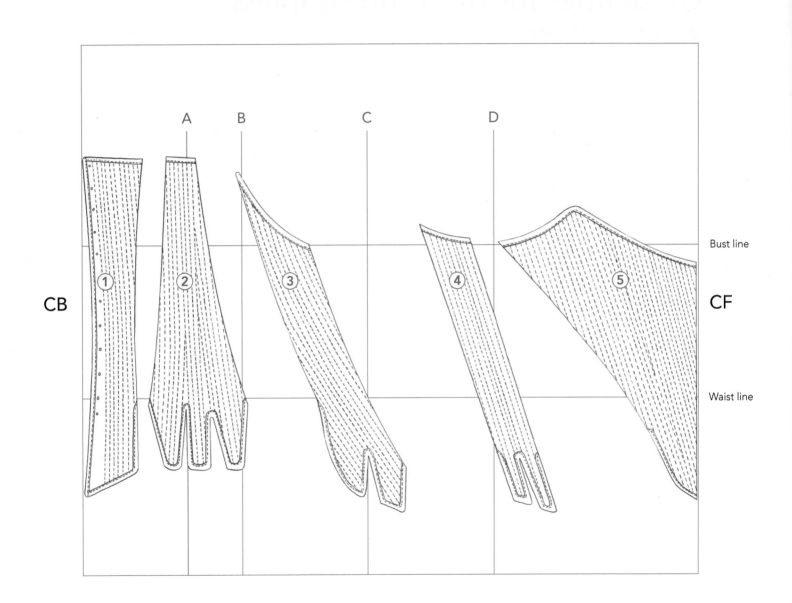

CB

CF

A   B   C   D

Bust line

Waist line

① ② ③ ④ ⑤

Guidelines for the 1760 strapless stays pattern

Trace and separate the female basic block pattern following the instructions in Chapter 5, 'Preparing the female basic block for your historic pattern'. Leave a gap of **30cm** between the basic block back side seam and basic block front side seam and number each lines.

Draw in the following additional guidelines

7 to **8**   **mid-hip** line

The **mid-hip** line lies half measurement (**3** to **5**) square across from the **CB** line to the **CF** line

9 to **10**   **high hip** line

The **high hip** line lies half measurement (**3** to **7**) square across from the **CB** line to the **CF** line

11 to **12** **lower mid-hip** line

The **lower mid-hip** line lies half measurement (**7** to **5**) square across from the **CB** line to the **CF** line

13 to **14** **across back** line

Line **B**   mark your traced female basic block back side seam line **B**

Line **D**   mark your traced female basic block front side seam line **D**

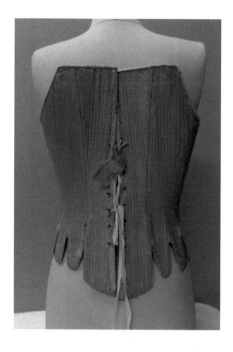

Back view and lacing detail of the 1760 buff strapless stays.

From the collections of Hampshire Cultural Trust.

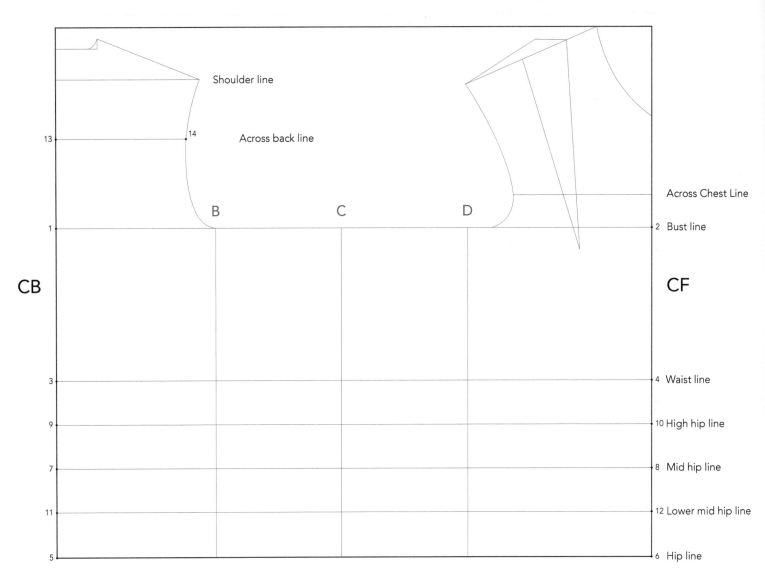

Shoulder line

Across back line

Across Chest Line

13 · · 14

B C D

1 · 2 Bust line

CB CF

3 · 4 Waist line

9 · 10 High hip line

7 · 8 Mid hip line

11 · 12 Lower mid hip line

5 · 6 Hip line

1760 strapless stays measurement tables

The tables below contain measurements for each pattern piece. Find the **bust** and **waist** measurements that are the closest to that of your model. The calculation for the size of each panel is recorded horizontally to these measurements.

1760 strapless stays measurement table for the bust

Bust measurement	Reduced bust measurement	Half reduced bust measurement	Panel 1	Panel 2	Panel 3	Panel 4	Panel 5
80cm	78cm	39cm	5.2cm	4.5cm	5.2cm	4.5cm	19.6cm
82cm	80cm	40cm	5.4cm	4.6cm	5.4cm	4.6cm	20cm
86cm	84cm	42cm	5.6cm	5cm	5.6cm	4.8cm	21cm
90cm	88cm	44cm	5.9cm	5.2cm	5.9cm	5cm	22cm
94cm	92cm	46cm	6.2cm	5.4cm	6.2cm	5.2cm	23cm
100cm	98cm	49cm	6.6cm	5.7cm	6.6cm	5.6cm	24.5cm
106cm	104cm	52cm	7cm	6cm	7cm	6cm	26cm
112cm	110cm	55cm	7.4cm	6.5cm	7.4cm	6.2cm	27.5cm
118cm	116cm	58cm	7.7cm	7cm	7.7cm	6.6cm	29cm
124cm	122cm	61cm	8.2cm	7.3cm	8cm	7cm	30.5cm

1760 strapless stays measurement table for the waist

Full waist measurement	Reduced waist measurement	Half reduced waist measurement	Panel 1	Panel 2	Panel 3	Panel 4	Panel 5
42cm	82cm	56cm	4.3cm	6.2cm	62cm	57cm	28.5cm
64cm	59cm	29.5cm	4.3cm	8.7cm	5.7cm	4.4cm	6.4cm
68cm	63cm	31.5cm	4.5cm	9.7cm	5.9cm	4.6cm	6.8cm
72cm	67cm	33.5cm	4.8cm	10.3cm	6.2cm	4.8cm	7.4cm
76cm	71cm	35.5cm	5.2cm	11cm	6.5cm	5cm	7.8cm
82cm	77cm	38.5cm	5.6cm	12cm	7cm	5.4cm	8.5cm
88cm	83cm	41.5cm	6cm	13cm	7.7cm	5.8cm	9cm
94cm	89cm	44.5cm	6.5cm	14cm	8.2cm	6cm	9.8cm
100cm	95cm	47.5cm	7.1cm	14.8cm	8.7cm	6.4cm	10.5cm
104cm	99cm	49.5cm	7.4cm	15.3cm	9cm	6.8cm	11cm

Create a table of measurements for your model

Create an individual table for your model
to isolate the specific measurements
required to draft your historical pattern.
See example table below.

1760 strapless stays individual measurement table example

Size	Full measurement	Reduced measurement	Half reduced measurement	Panel 1	Panel 2	Panel 3	Panel 4	Panel 5
Bust	90cm	88cm	44cm	5.9cm	5.2cm	5.9cm	5cm	22cm
Waist	68cm	63cm	31.5cm	4.5cm	9.7cm	5.9cm	4.6cm	6.8cm

1760 strapless stays detail showing the repairs to the centre front panel.

From the collections of Hampshire Cultural Trust.

Begin plotting the 1760 strapless stays onto your traced basic block pattern

Panel 1

3 to 15   1cm

15 to 16   **waist** measurement

1 to 17   0.7cm

17 to 18   **bust** measurement

17 to 15   connect with a temporary straight line

18 to 16   connect with a temporary straight line

Panel 5

4 to 19   **waist** measurement

2 to 20   **bust** measurement

20 to 19   connect with a temporary straight line

Panel 3

21   lies at the junction of the **waist**line and line **C**

21 to 22   **waist** measurement to the left of line **C**

23   lies at the junction of the **bust** line and line **B**

23 to 24   1.2cm to the right of line **B**

24 to 25   **bust** measurement

24 to 22   connect with a temporary straight line

25 to 21   connect with a temporary straight line

Draw in the following additional guideline

Line **A**   on the **waist**line mark one third measurement (**16** to **22**) square up to the **shoulder** line and down to **hip** line

Note: The position of line **A** will differ slightly depending on the size of your basic block pattern

Panel 2

26 to 27   **waist** measurement distribute equally either side of line **A**

28 to 29   **bust** measurement distribute three fifths to the left of line **A** and two fifths to the right of line **A**

28 to 26   connect with a temporary straight line

29 to 27   connect with a temporary straight line

Panel 4

30 to 31   **waist** measurement distribute equally either side of line **D**

32   lies at the junction of the **bust** line and line **D**

32 to 33   3.8cm to the left of line **D**

33 to 34   **bust** measurement

34 to 30   connect with a straight line

33 to 31   connect with a straight line

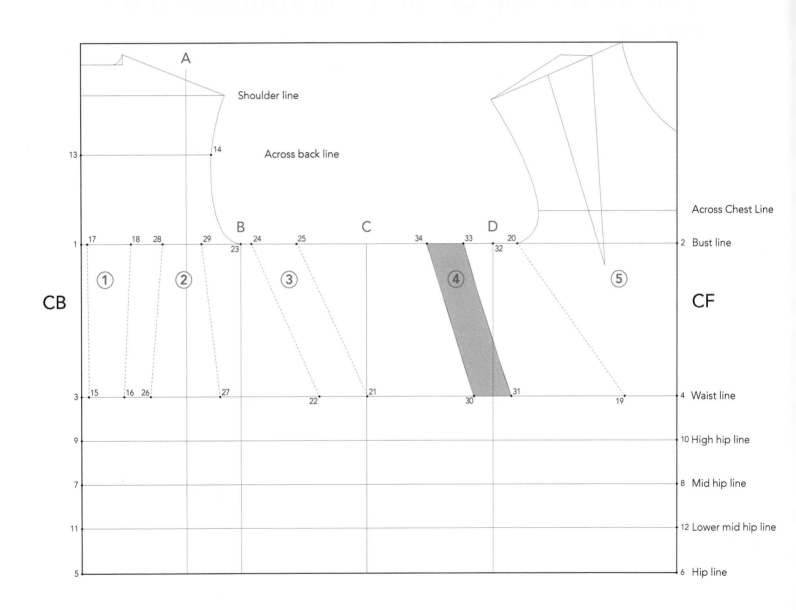

Extend the top of the 1760 strapless stays pattern

Panel 1

13 to **35**	**0.7cm** on the **across back** line
35 to **36**	one third measurement (**13** to **14**) connect with a straight line

35 through **17** to **15** connect with a very slight concave curve using the diagram as a guide

16 to **37**	half measurement (**16** to **18**)
37 to **38**	square across **0.5cm**

36 through **38** to **16** connect with a continuous line using the diagram as a guide. Note: this line will not go through point **18**

Panel 2

39 to **40**	half measurement (**35** to **36**) on the **across back** line – distribute two thirds to the left of line **A** and one third to the right of line **A**
39 to **28**	connect with a temporary straight line
40 to **29**	connect with a temporary straight line
39 to **26**	connect with a very shallow concave curve using the diagram as a guide (this line may not go through point **28**)

Ensure that line (**26** to **39**) is the same length as (**16** through **38** to **36**) – adjust if necessary

40 to **41**	**0.8cm**
27 to **42**	half measurement (**27** to **29**)
42 to **43**	square across **0.3cm**

41 through **43** to **27** connect with a shallow concave curve using the diagram as a guide – this may not go through point **29**

39 to **41**	connect with a straight line

Panel 3

Extend line **B** to level with the **across back** line

Extend the **across back** line (**13** to **14**) to line **B** – where these lines meet is point **44**

22 to **45**	half measurement (**22** to **24**)
45 to **46**	square across **0.3cm**

44 through **24** and **46** to **22** connect with a continuous convex curve using the diagram as a guide

Measure line **27** through **43** to **41** on **Panel 2** transfer this measurement to **Panel 3** from point **22** through **46** and **24** to find point **47**

Extend temporary line (**21** to **25**) by **1.2cm** beyond point **25** to find point **48**

47 to **48**	connect with a temporary straight line
48 to **49**	one third measurement (**47** to **48**)
49 to **50**	square down **1cm**

47 through **50** to **48** connect with a concave curve

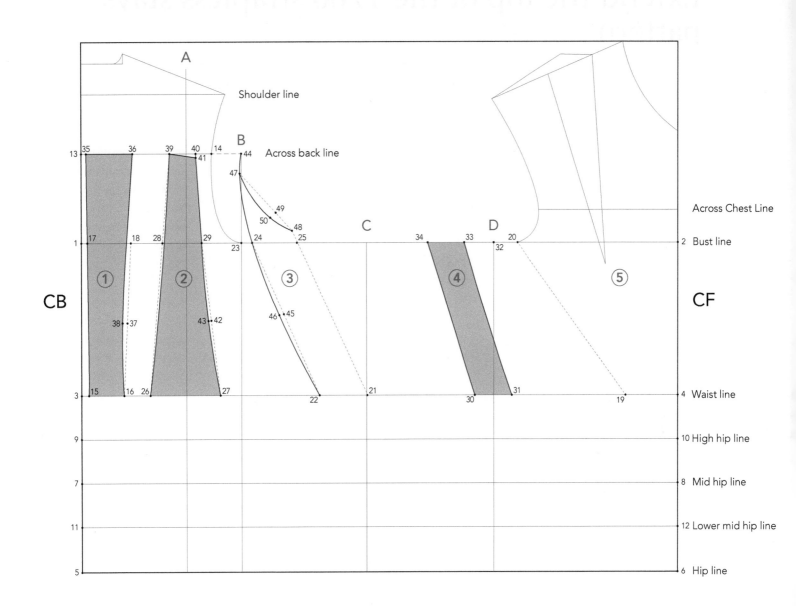

Extend the top of the 1760 strapless stays pattern

Panel 4

Measure temporary line **21** through **25** to **48** on **Panel 3** transfer this measurement to **Panel 4** from point **30** through **34** and extend line to find point **51**

Extend line (**31** to **33**) by **0.7cm** to find point **52**

51 to **52**	connect with a shallow concave curve

Panel 5

19 to **53**	one third measurement (**19** to **20**)
53 to **54**	square across **0.3cm**
20 to **55**	two fifths measurement (**2** to **20**)

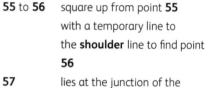

55 to **56**	square up from point **55** with a temporary line to the **shoulder** line to find point **56**
57	lies at the junction of the **across chest** line and line (**55** to **56**)
57 to **58**	**1.2cm** on the **across chest** line towards the **armhole** connect with a straight line
20 to **58**	connect with a shallow concave curve using the basic block front **armhole** as a guide
2 to **59**	**1cm** on **CF** line
57 to **59**	connect with a very shallow concave curve

Round off the corners at points **57** and **58**

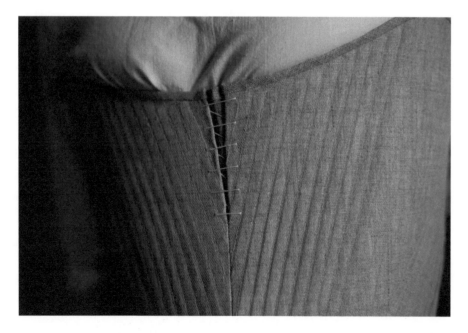

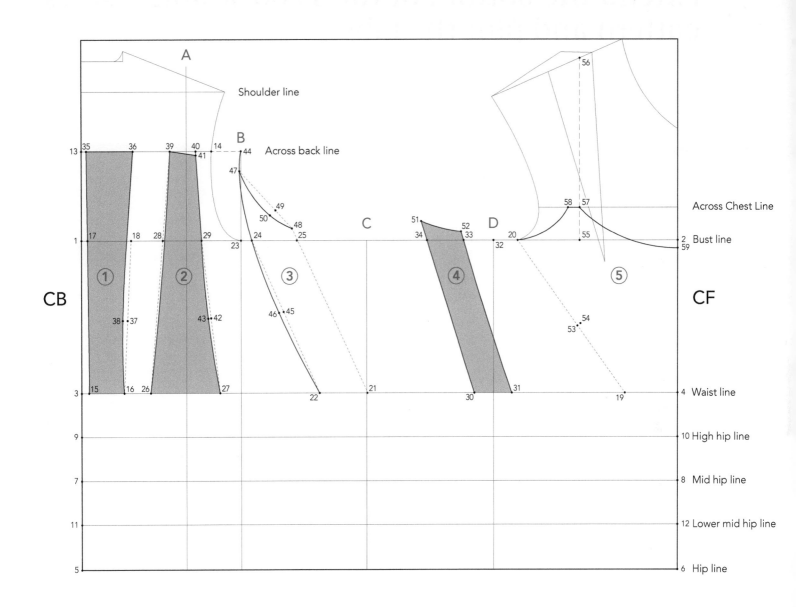

CB

CF

A

Shoulder line

B — Across back line

C

D

Across Chest Line

Bust line

Waist line

High hip line

Mid hip line

Lower mid hip line

Hip line

① ② ③ ④ ⑤

Extend the bottom of the 1760 strapless stays pattern and plot the tabs

Panel 1

7 to **60**	measurement (**15** to **16**) **waist** plus **1.5cm**
60 to **61**	square up from point **60** with a temporary line to the **high hip** line to find point **61**
61 to **62**	half measurement (**60** to **61**)
15 to **7**	connect with a shallow concave curve
16 to **62**	connect with a straight line
7 to **62**	connect with a straight line

Round off the corners at points **7** and **62**

Panel 2

26 to **63**	square down from point **26** with a temporary line to the **mid-hip** line to find point **63**
27 to **64**	square down from point **27** with a temporary line to the **mid-hip** line to find point **64**
63 to **65**	one quarter measurement (**26** to **63**)
64 to **66**	**2cm**
65 to **66**	connect with a temporary straight line
65 to **67**	**1cm**

66 to **68**	**0.7cm**
26 to **67**	connect with a straight line
27 to **68**	connect with a straight line
67 to **69**	one fifth measurement (**67** to **68**)
68 to **70**	one fifth measurement (**67** to **68**) plus **0.5cm**
69 to **71**	**0.5cm**
71 to **72**	one fifth measurement (**65** to **66**) plus **0.8cm**

Divide measurement (**26** to **27**) by **3** to find points **73** and **74**

73 to **73a**	square down **0.5cm**

73a to **69**	connect with a straight line
73a to **71**	connect with a straight line
74 to **72**	connect with a straight line
74 to **70**	connect with a straight line
67 to **69**	connect with a straight line
71 to **72**	connect with a straight line
70 to **68**	connect with a straight line

Round off the corners at points **67**, **69**, **71**, **72**, **70** and **68**

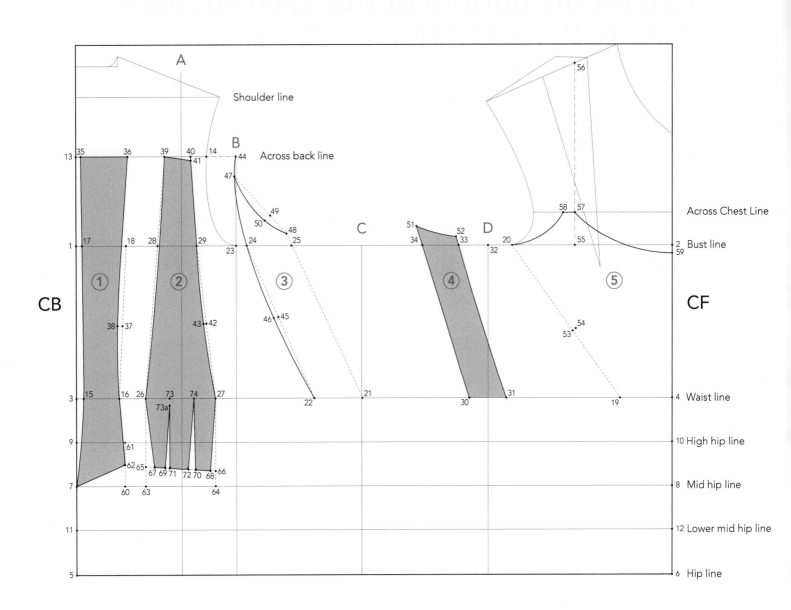

Extend the bottom of the 1760 strapless stays pattern and plot the tabs

Panel 3

22 to **75**	square down from point **22** with a temporary line to the **mid-hip** line to find point **75**
76	lies at the junction of the **high hip** line and line (**22** to **75**)
76 to **77**	**1cm** on the **high hip** line

Extend temporary line (**48** through **25** to **21**) to the **high hip** line to find point **78**

Connect and extend line (**48** through **25** to **21**) with a shallow concave curve to approximately **1cm** to the right of point **78** and **1.5cm** beyond the **high hip** line to find point **79**

79 to **80**	square down from point **79** with a temporary line to the **lower mid-hip** to find point **80**
81	lies at the junction of line (**79** to **80**) and the **mid-hip** line
81 to **82**	half measurement (**80** to **81**)
75 to **83**	one third measurement (**75** to **81**) on the **mid-hip** line

83 to **82**	connect with a temporary straight line
83 to **84**	**1.5cm** on the **mid-hip** line

22 through **77** to **83** connect with a slight convex curve

85	lies at the junction of line (**48** through **25** and **21** to **79**) and the **high hip** line
85 to **86**	two fifths measurement (**77** to **85**)
83 to **87**	two fifths measurement (**83** to **82**)

86 to **84**	connect with a straight line
86 to **87**	connect with a straight line
83 to **84**	connect with a straight line
87 to **82**	connect with a straight line

Round off the tabs at points **83**, **84**, **87** and **82**

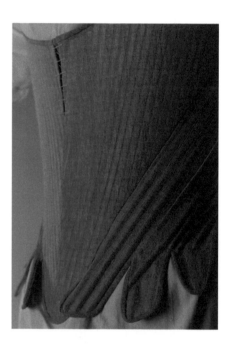

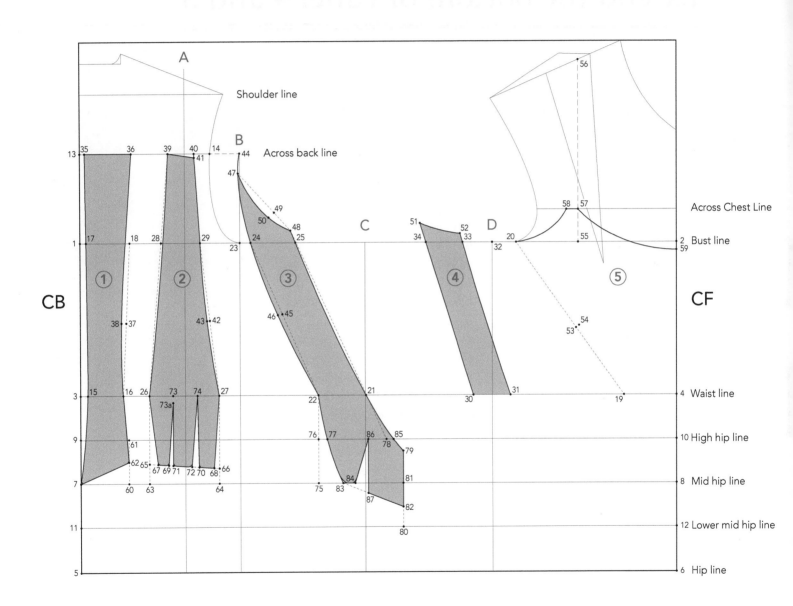

A

Shoulder line

B

Across back line

Across Chest Line

C

D

CB

CF

Bust line

① ② ③ ④ ⑤

Waist line

High hip line

Mid hip line

Lower mid hip line

Hip line

Extend the bottom of Panel 4 and 5

Panel 4

Extend line **51** through **34** to **30** to the **lower mid-hip** line to find point **88**

Extend line **52** through **33** to **31** to the **lower mid-hip** line to find point **89**

Measure line **48** through **25, 21** and **85** to **79** on **Panel 3** transfer this measurement to **Panel 4** from point **51** through **34** and **30** to find point **90**

Measure line **79** through **81** to **82** on **Panel 3** transfer this measurement to **Panel 4** from point **90** to find point **91**

89 to **92**	**1cm**
91 to **92**	connect with a temporary straight line

Note: small sizes may wish to leave **panel 4** as one tab instead of splitting it into two, if so stop **panel 4** instructions once you have connected points (**91** to **92**)

92 to **93**	is the same measurement as (**90** to **91**)
90 to **93**	connect with a temporary straight line

90 to **94**	half measurement (**90** to **93**)
91 to **95**	half measurement (**91** to **92**) minus **0.3cm**
92 to **96**	half measurement (**91** to **92**) minus **0.3cm**
94 to **95**	connect with a straight line
94 to **96**	connect with a straight line
91 to **95**	connect with a straight line
96 to **92**	connect with a straight line

Round off the tabs at points **91**, **95**, **96** and **92**

Panel 5

8 to **97**	one third measurement (**8** to **12**) on the **CF** line
10 to **98**	two thirds measurement (**4** to **19**) on the **high hip** line
8 to **99**	half measurement (**10** to **98**) on the **mid hip** line

20 through **54** and **19** to **98** connect with a shallow concave curve

98 through **99** and **97** connect with a convex curve

Ensure that these two curves connect smoothly

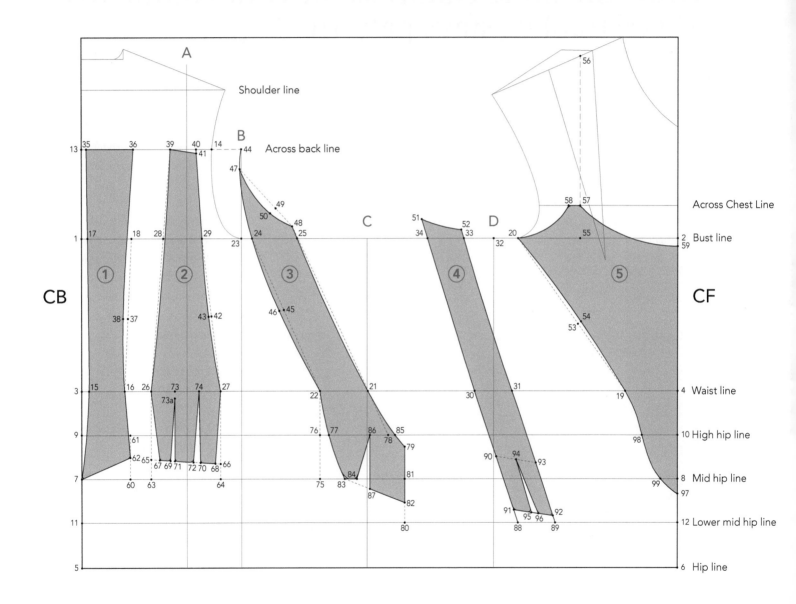

Shoulder line

Across back line

Across Chest Line

Bust line

CB

CF

Waist line

High hip line

Mid hip line

Lower mid hip line

Hip line

Draw the bone channels on your completed 1760 strapless stays pattern

Using the diagram as a guide draw the bone channels for each panel on your completed pattern. The number of bones will differ depending on the size of your stays and the rigidity that you require. The bone channels in this pattern are **0.7cm**

wide to fit a bone that is **0.5cm** wide; this is closer to the original garment and suits the style and period of the stays. These can be amended to wider bone channels and bones if required. At the centre back there are two bone channels that are **1cm**

wide with a central eyelet channel that is **1.3cm** wide on both sides for lacing up the stays.

When tracing your pattern it is vital that you note where your panels will join when sewn together. You may want to replace the numbers with a common letter or number to simplify the process of matching these. The tabs are left open to spread over the hips.

Panel 1 points **36** to **16** will be sewn to **Panel 2** points **39** to **26**

Panel 2 points **41** to **27** will be sewn to **Panel 3** points **47** to **22**

Panel 3 points **48** to **79** will be sewn to **Panel 4** points **51** to **90**

Panel 4 points **52** to **93** will be sewn to **Panel 5** points **20** to just below point **98**

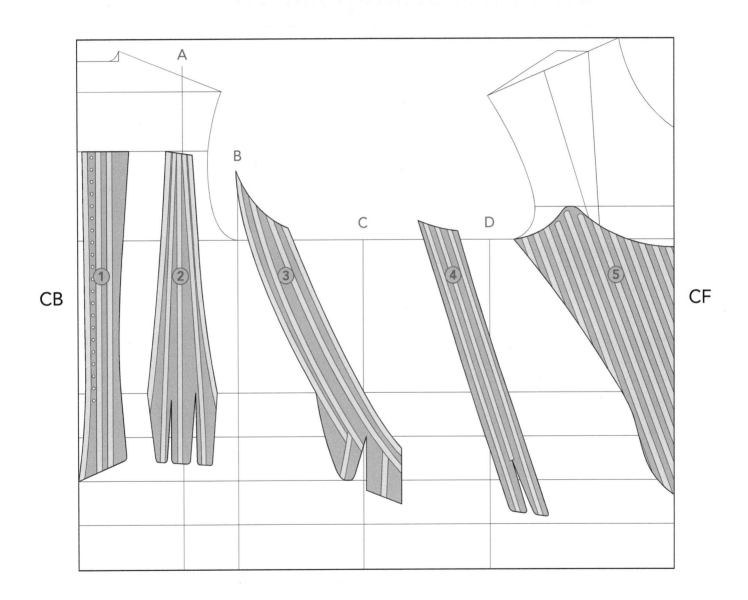

1760 stays optional strap pattern

A guide to the length of your shoulder strap

Take the following measurement from your pattern

Panel 2

Point **39** on the **shoulder** line of your stays pattern square up to the mid-point of the back **shoulder** of the traced female basic block pattern

Panel 4

Point **57** on the front of your stays pattern to point **56** on the front **shoulder** of your traced female basic block

These two measurements added together will give you an approximate length for your strap, but will need adjusting at the fitting stage as the straps go across the top of the arm.

1 to **2**   strap length (calculated from your pattern) plus **3cm**

1 to **3**   square up **6cm** with a temporary line

3 to **4**   square across **3.3cm** with a temporary line

4 to **1**   connect with a straight line

2 to **5**   square up **2.5cm**

4 to **5**   connect with a shallow concave curve using the diagram as a guide

Round off the end of the strap at points **1** and **5**

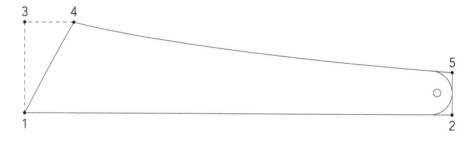

11 1830–45 buff corded corset

1830–45 buff corded corset

This particular corset is thought to date between 1830 and 1845; the exact date is unknown. The design of the corset is transitional, it has retained the long line from the previous decade but now has four panels that act as seams to give shaping down the back and through the bust line. The corset remains soft, with cording rather than bone channels to support its structure and shaping. The straps are sewn to the inside of the back and tied at the front. These lie across the tops of the arms to allow for the wide fashionable neckline of the period.

The 1830–45 corset is part of a collection held by Hampshire Cultural Trust at Chilcombe House Museum resource and learning centre. It is made from two layers of buff cotton twill and was probably constructed at home. It is all hand sewn with even neat stitches between the rows of cording; the top edge is trimmed with cotton tape. The corset would have been close fitting and although only corded would have provided the ability to control and shape the figure. It is relatively small, with a 81cm (32 inches) bust, 66cm (26 inches) waist and 94cm (37 inches) hip measurement; the centre front is 40.6cm (16 inches) and the centre back is 41.8cm (16.5 inches) long.

I have included the 1830–45 corset pattern as it is from a period when very view examples of underwear survive. It creates the very wide neckline and longline body and will work effectively under dresses of this period. For this pattern I have kept the same number of cording channels as the original corset, although larger sizes will need to add more cording channels. If greater control is required, additional bones can be added to each seam. Although the original does not have any gathering across the bust, this could be added and used to shape the neckline of the corset across the bust.

When constructing this corset I suggest that you include wider seam allowances and check your pattern panel sizes against your sewn and corded pieces, as they can shrink slightly when the cording is added.

Opposite: 1830–45 buff corded corset.

From the collections of Hampshire Cultural Trust.

Original 1830–45 buff corded corset pattern

The lines on the 1830–45 historical corset pattern diagram opposite are a guide for drafting the new pattern onto the female basic block. The approximate position of the **point to point** line, **waist**line and **hip** line are shown on the diagram, it is also labelled with the **CB** and **CF** and lines **B** and **D** which are additional guidelines for the position of **Panel 2** and **Panel 3**.

The front and back views of the original 1830–45 four panel corset shows the seam lines, cording channels and front busk.

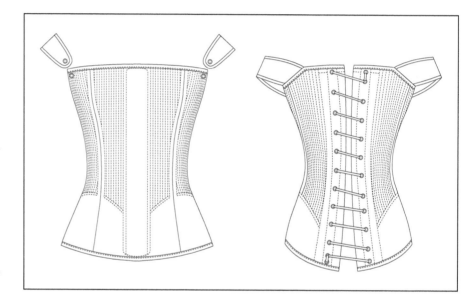

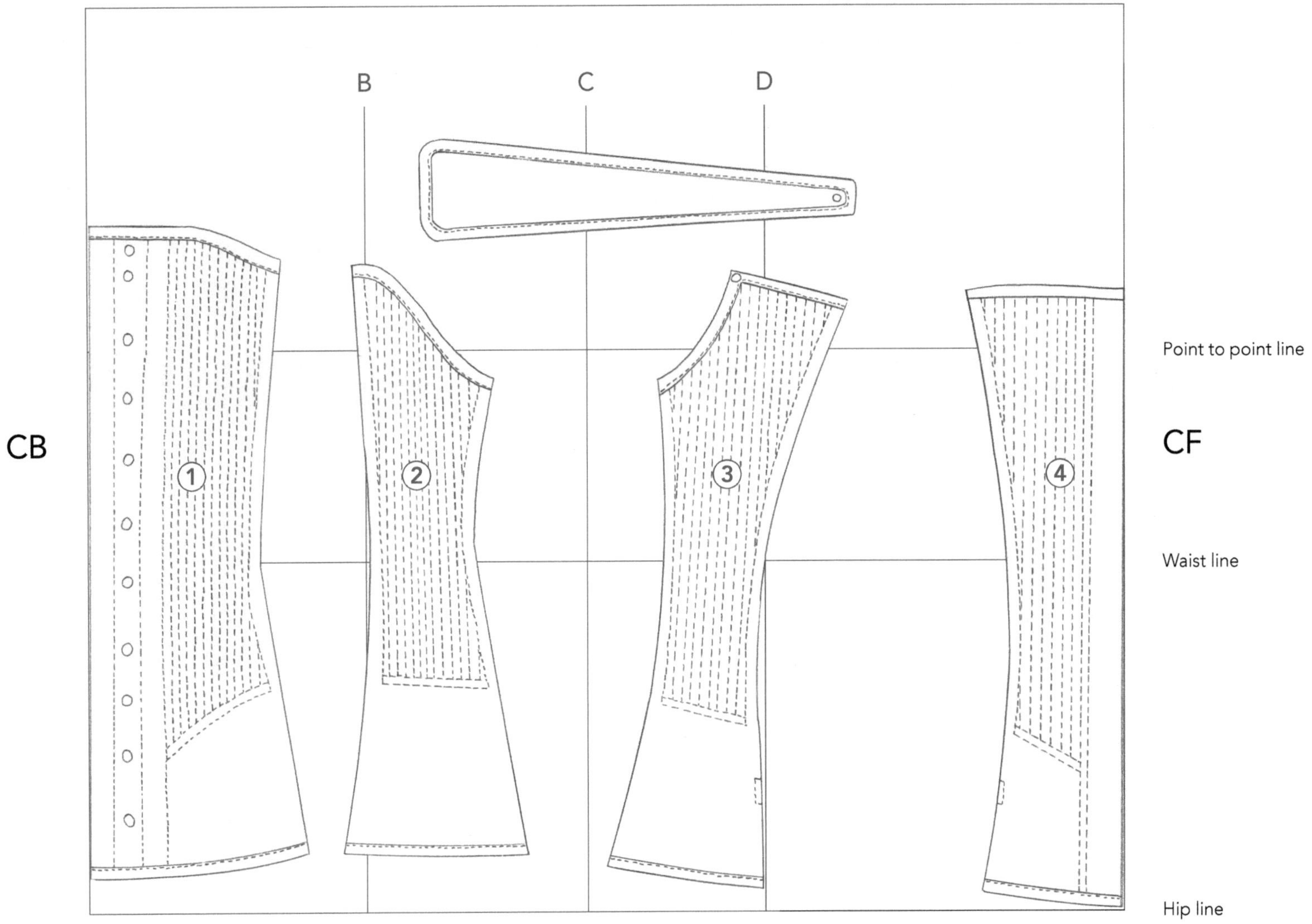

B   C   D

Point to point line

CB   CF

Waist line

① ② ③ ④

Hip line

Guidelines for the 1830–45 buff corded corset pattern

Trace and separate the female basic block pattern following the instructions in Chapter 5, 'Preparing the female basic block for your historic pattern'. Leave a gap of **30cm** between the basic block back side seam and basic block front side seam and number each line.

Draw in the following additional guidelines

7 to **8**   **point to point** line

The **point to point** line lies at the base of the **bust** dart square across from the **CB** line to the **CF** line

9 to **10**   **mid hip** line

The **mid-hip** line lies half measurement (**3** to **5**) square across from the **CB** line to the **CF** line

11 to **12**   **lower mid-hip** line

The **lower mid-hip** line lies half measurement (**9** to **5**) square across from the **CB** line to the **CF** line

13 to **14 across chest** line

Line **B**   mark your traced female basic block back side seam line **B**

Line **D**   mark your traced female basic block front side seam line **D**

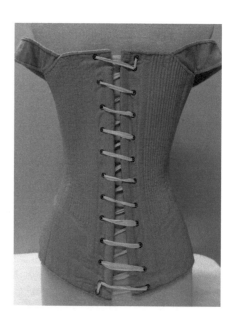

Back view of the 1830–45 corset showing the applied cording channels and back lacing panels.

From the collections of Hampshire Cultural Trust.

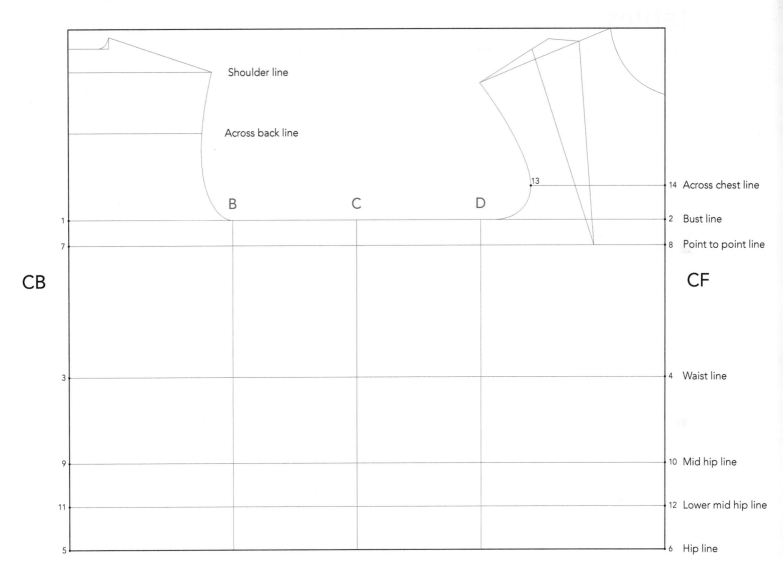

Shoulder line

Across back line

13

B   C   D

CB   CF

14 Across chest line
2 Bust line
8 Point to point line

1
7

3

9

11

5

4 Waist line

10 Mid hip line

12 Lower mid hip line

6 Hip line

1830–45 buff corded corset measurement tables

The tables below contain measurements for each pattern piece. Find the **bust**, **waist** and **hip** measurements that are the closest to that of your model. The calculation for the size of each panel is recorded horizontally to these measurements.

1830 buff corded corset measurement table for the bust

Bust measurement	Reduced bust measurement	Half reduced bust measurement	Panel 1	Panel 2	Panel 3	Panel 4
80cm	78cm	39cm	11.7cm	8.6cm	9.7cm	9cm
82cm	80cm	40cm	12cm	8.8cm	10cm	9.2cm
86cm	84cm	42cm	12.6cm	9.2cm	10.5cm	9.7cm
90cm	88cm	44cm	13.2cm	9.7cm	11cm	10.1cm
94cm	92cm	46cm	13.8cm	10.1cm	11.5cm	10.6cm
100cm	98cm	49cm	14.7cm	10.8cm	12.2cm	11.3cm
106cm	104cm	52cm	15.6cm	11.4cm	13cm	12cm
112cm	110cm	55cm	16.5cm	12.1cm	13.8cm	12.6cm
118cm	116cm	58cm	17.4cm	12.8cm	14.5cm	13.3cm
124cm	122cm	61cm	18.3cm	13.4cm	15.3cm	14cm

1830 buff corded corset measurement table for the waist

Full waist measurement	Reduced waist measurement	Half reduced waist measurement	Panel 1	Panel 2	Panel 3	Panel 4
62cm	57cm	28.5cm	10cm	6.2cm	5.7cm	6.6cm
64cm	59cm	29.5cm	10.3cm	6.5cm	5.9cm	6.8cm
68cm	63cm	31.5cm	11cm	6.9cm	6.3cm	7.3cm
72cm	67cm	33.5cm	11.7cm	7.3cm	6.7cm	7.8cm
76cm	71cm	35.5cm	12.4cm	7.8cm	7.1cm	8.2cm
82cm	77cm	38.5cm	13.4cm	8.5cm	7.7cm	8.9cm
88cm	83cm	41.5cm	14.5cm	9.1cm	8.3cm	9.6cm
94cm	89cm	44.5cm	15.5cm	9.7cm	9cm	10.3cm
100cm	95cm	47.5cm	16.6cm	10.4cm	9.5cm	11cm
104cm	99cm	49.5cm	17.3cm	10.8cm	10cm	11.4cm

1830 buff corded corset measurement table for the hips

Full hip measurement	Half hip measurement	Panel 1	Panel 2	Panel 3	Panel 4
84cm	42cm	13.1cm	10.4cm	10.2cm	8.3cm
88cm	44cm	13.7cm	11cm	10.6cm	8.7cm
92cm	46cm	14.4cm	11.4cm	11.1cm	9.1cm
96cm	48cm	15cm	11.9cm	11.6cm	9.5cm
100cm	50cm	15.6cm	12.4cm	12.1cm	9.9cm
106cm	53cm	16.5cm	13.2cm	12.8cm	10.5cm
112cm	56cm	17.5cm	13.9cm	13.5cm	11.1cm
118cm	59cm	18.4cm	14.6cm	14.3cm	11.7cm
124cm	62cm	19.3cm	15.4cm	15cm	12.3cm
130cm	65cm	20.3cm	16.2cm	15.7cm	12.8cm

Create a table of measurements for your model

Create an individual table for your model
to isolate the specific measurements
required to draft your historical pattern.
See example table below.

1830 buff corded corset individual measurement table

Size	Full measurement	Reduced measurement	Half reduced measurement	Panel 1	Panel 2	Panel 3	Panel 4
Bust	90cm	88cm	44cm	13.2cm	9.7cm	11cm	10.1cm
Waist	68cm	63cm	31.5cm	11cm	6.9cm	6.3cm	7.3cm
Hip	100cm		50cm	15.6cm	12.4cm	12.1cm	9.9cm

Begin plotting the 1830–45 buff corded corset onto your traced basic block pattern

When drafting the **1830–45** corset pattern the **bust** measurements are plotted onto the **point to point** line and the **hip** measurements are plotted on the **lower mid hip** line. When this does not apply it is highlighted within the pattern instructions.

Panel 1

3 to **15**	**waist** measurement
7 to **16**	**bust** measurement
11 to **17**	**hip** measurement
16 to **15**	connect with a temporary straight line
15 to **17**	connect with a very slight convex curve

Panel 4

4 to **18**	**waist** measurement
8 to **19**	**bust** measurement
12 to **20**	**hip** measurement
19 to **18**	connect with a temporary straight line
18 to **20**	connect with a straight line

Panel 2

21	lies at the junction of the **waist**line and line **B**
21 to **22**	**waist** measurement to the right of line **B**
23	lies at the junction of the **point to point** line and line **B**
23 to **24**	**1.5cm** to the left of line **B**
24 to **25**	**bust** measurement
26	lies at the junction of the **lower mid hip** line and line **B**
26 to **27**	**1cm** to the left of line **B**
27 to **28**	**hip** measurement
24 to **21**	connect with a temporary straight line
21 to **27**	connect with a very slight convex curve
25 to **22**	connect with a very shallow concave curve
22 to **28**	connect with a very shallow concave curve

Panel 3

29	lies at the junction of the **waist**line and line **D**
29 to **30**	**waist** measurement to the left of line **D**
31 to **32**	**bust** measurement distribute three quarters of the **bust** measurement left of line **D** and one quarter of the **bust** measurement to the right of line **D**
33	lies at the junction of the **lower mid hip** line and line **D**
33 to **34**	**1cm** to the right of line **D**
34 to **35**	**hip** measurement
31 to **30**	connect with a very shallow concave curve
30 to **35**	connect with a very shallow concave curve
32 to **29**	connect with a temporary straight line
29 to **34**	connect with a straight line

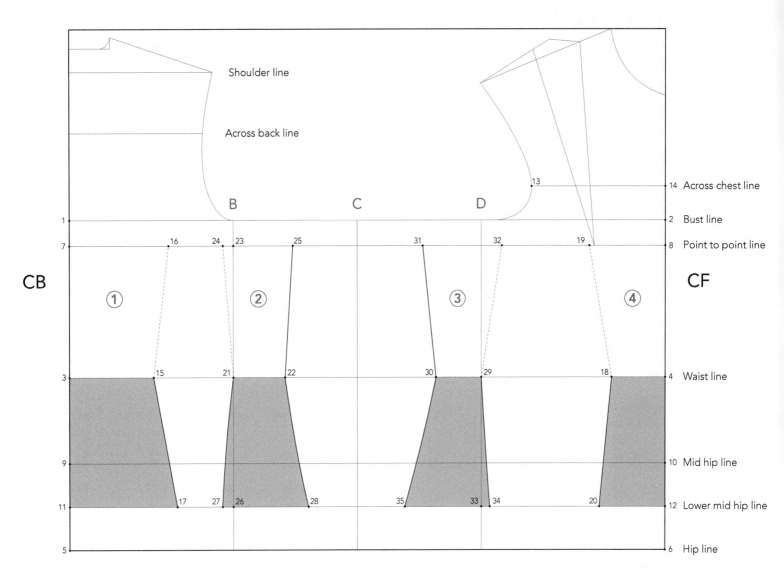

Extend the top of the 1830–45 buff corded corset pattern

Panel 1

36	lies at the junction of the **CB** line and the **across chest** line
1 to **37**	half measurement (**1** to **36**) plus **1cm**
37 to **38**	square across from point **37** with a temporary line to the **armhole** to find point **38**
16 to **39**	extend line (**15** to **16**) to temporary line (**37** to **38**) – where these lines meet is point **39**
39 to **40**	one quarter measurement (**39** to **16**)
15 to **41**	one quarter measurement (**15** to **16**)
41 to **42**	square across **0.3cm**

40 through **42** to **15** connect with a very shallow concave curve

Note: this will not go through point **16**

Panel 2

Measure temporary line **15** through **16** to **40** on **Panel 1** transfer measurement to **Panel 2** from point **21** through **24** to find point **43**

21 to **44**	one quarter measurement (**21** to **24**)
44 to **45**	square across **0.3cm**

43 through **45** to **21** connect with a shallow concave curve

Note: this will not go through point **24**

Ensure that line (**21** through **45** to **43**) is the same length as (**15** through **42** to **40**) – adjust if necessary

Panel 3

Measure line **22** to **25** on **Panel 2** and **30** to **31** on **Panel 3** and ensure that they are the same length – adjust if necessary

31 to **46**	two fifths measurement (**31** to **32**)

Extend the **across chest** line (**13** to **14**) to level with point **46**

46 to **47**	square up from point **46** with a temporary line to the extended **across chest** line – where these lines meet is point **47**
47 to **48**	extend line (**46** to **47**) **1.5cm** to find point **48**
47 to **49**	four fifths measurement (**31** to **32**)
49 to **32**	connect with a temporary straight line

32 to **50**	half measurement (**29** to **32**)
50 to **51**	square across **0.5cm**
32 to **52**	half measurement (**32** to **49**)
52 to **53**	square across **0.3cm**

49 through **53**, **32**, **51** to **29** connect with a continuous curve using the diagram as a guide

Panel 4

Measure temporary line **29** through **50**, **32** and **52** to **49** on **Panel 3** transfer measurement to **Panel 4** from point **18** through **19** and extend line to find point **54**

18 to **55**	half measurement (**18** to **19**)
55 to **56**	square across **0.5cm**
54 to **57**	half measurement (**54** to **19**)
57 to **58**	square across **0.3cm**

54 through **58**, **19** and **56** to **18** connect with a continuous curve using the diagram as a guide

Ensure that line (**54** through **58**, **19** and **56** to **18**) is the same length as (**49** through **53**, **32** and **51** to **29**) – adjust if necessary

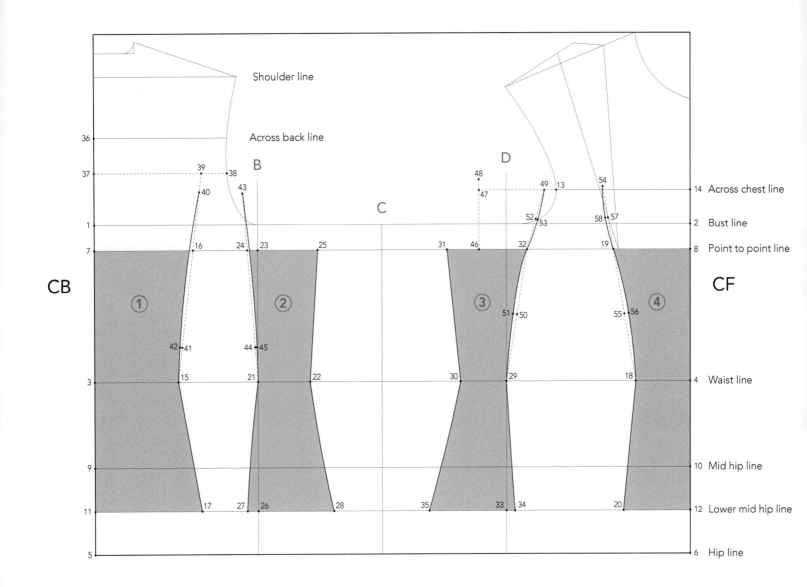

Shoulder line

Across back line

B

D

C

36

37

39

38

40

43

48

47

49

13

54

14 Across chest line

52

53

58

57

1

2 Bust line

7

16

24

23

25

31

46

32

19

8 Point to point line

CB

CF

①

②

③

④

51

50

55

56

42

41

44

45

15

21

22

30

29

18

4 Waist line

3

9

10 Mid hip line

11

17

27

26

28

35

33

34

20

12 Lower mid hip line

5

6 Hip line

Extend the bottom of your 1830–45 buff corded corset pattern

Panel 1

11 to **59**   half measurement (**11** to **5**) on the **CB** line

17 to **60** extend line (**15** to **17**) by **0.5cm** to find point **60**

Panel 2

Measure line **15** through **17** to **60** on **Panel 1** transfer to **Panel 2** from point **21** through **27** to find point **61**

28 to **62**   extend line (**22** to **28**) by **1cm** to find point **62**

Panel 3

Measure line **22** through **28** to **62** on **Panel 2** transfer measurement to **Panel 3** from point **30** through **35** to find point **63**

34 to **64**   extend line (**29** to **34**) by **2.5cm** to find point **64**

Panel 4

Measure line **29** through **34** to **64** on **Panel 3** transfer measurement to **Panel 4** from point **18** through **20** to find point **65**

6 to **66**   **1.3cm** on **CF** line

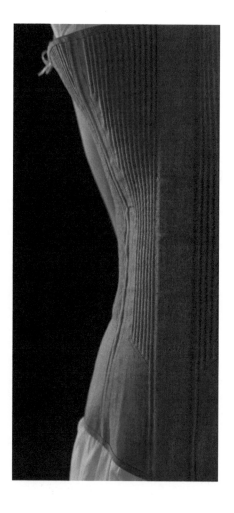

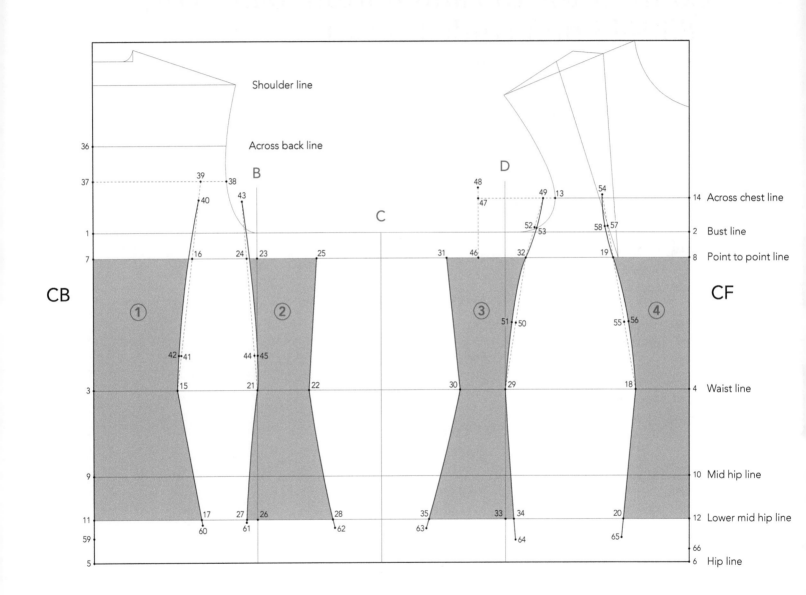

Connect the top and bottom panels of 1830–45 buff corded corset

1830–45 corset top line

Panel 1

37 to **67**	half measurement (**37** to **39**) plus **1cm**
67 to **40**	connect with a temporary straight line
67 to **68**	one quarter measurement (**67** to **40**)
40 to **69**	one quarter measurement (**67** to **40**)
69 to **70**	square down **0.3cm**

37 to **67**, **68** and **70** to **40** connect with a continuous line using the diagram as a guide

Panel 2

43 to **25**	connect with a temporary straight line
43 to **71**	square across **2cm** from point **43** to find point **71** – this may not hit line **B**
25 to **72**	half measurement (**43** to **25**) minus **1cm**
72 to **73**	half measurement (**25** to **72**)
73 to **74**	square down **1cm**

43 through **71**, **72** and **74** to **25** connect with a continuous curve using the diagram as a guide

Panel 3

48 to **31**	connect with a deep concave curve using the diagram as a guide
48 to **49**	connect with a slight convex curve

Panel 4

54 to **14**	connect with a slight convex curve

1830–45 corset bottom line

Panel 1

59 to **60** connect with a slight convex curve

Panel 2

61 to **62** connect with a very shallow concave curve

Panel 3

63 to **64** connect with a very shallow concave curve

Panel 4

65 to **66** connect with a slight convex curve

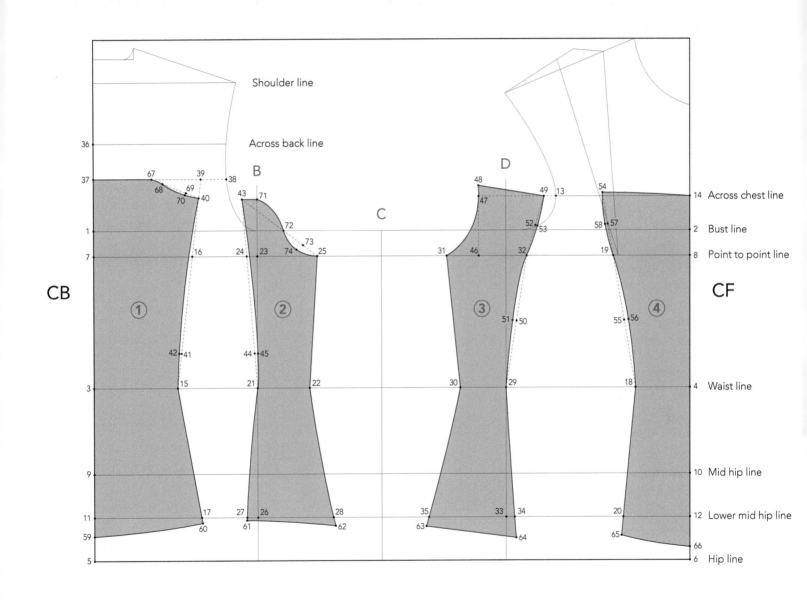

Shoulder line

Across back line

B

C

D

36

37

CB

CF

① ② ③ ④

Across chest line

Bust line

Point to point line

Waist line

Mid hip line

Lower mid hip line

Hip line

Plot the 1830–45 buff corset bodice shoulder strap pattern

A guide to the length of your strap

Take the following measurements from your pattern

Panel 1

Point **67** on the **shoulder** line of your stays pattern to the mid-point of the back **shoulder** of your traced female basic block pattern

Panel 3

Point **54** on the front of your corset pattern to the front **shoulder** of your traced female basic block pattern

These two measurements added together will give you an approximate strap length although these will need adjusting at the fitting stage

1 to 2	strap length (as calculated from your pattern) plus **5cm**
1 to 3	square up **6cm** from point **1** with a temporary line to find point **3**
3 to 4	square across **0.5cm** from point **3** to find point **4**
4 to 1	connect with a straight line

2 to 5	square up **2.5cm**
4 to 5	connect with a concave curve using the diagram as a guide
1 to 2	connect with a concave curve using the diagram as a guide

Round off the corners of the strap at points **2** and **5**

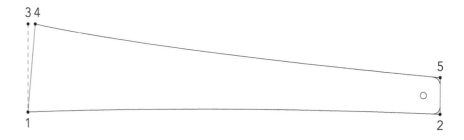

Draw the cording channels on your completed 1830–45 buff corded corset pattern

Use the diagram as a guide when drawing in your cording channels; these are **0.5cm** wide and cover the top half of the corset. The number of cording channels will depend on the size of your corset. At the centre back there are two bone channels of **1cm** wide and a central eyelet channel that is **1.3cm** wide on both sides for lacing up the corset. The front busk channel is **4cm** wide; this can be replaced with a smaller busk if required.

When tracing your pattern mark the number on each panel and the **waist** position to help you identify them accurately and align each piece when sewing your corset together. Each half of the corset connects in numerical order as they are seen on the pattern. The strap is completed before it is sewn to the corset on **panel 1** below points **67** to **40**.

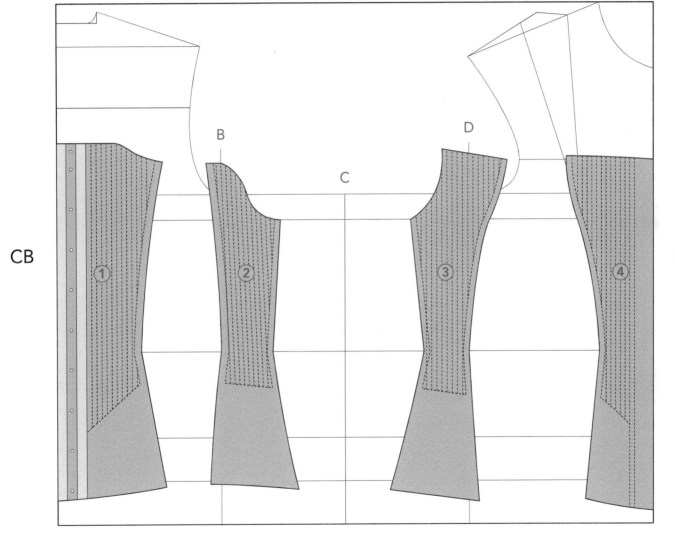

CB

CF

B

C

D

① ② ③ ④

12 1890 black cotton corset

1890 black cotton corset

This 1890 corset is part of a collection held at the Hereford Museum Resource and Learning Centre, Hereford, England and is made from black glazed cotton. The corset is lined with white cotton twill and the top and bottom edges are bound with cotton tape, it has only eight panels and is stiffened with spiral steels. The seams are machine sewn towards the outside of the corset and are covered with decorative fabric strips of pale pink blossom on a black background to create the bone channels. The top edge has a black and beige lace trim.

The 1890 corset is extremely small and may have been made for a young girl or very petite woman. It has a small 73.6cm (29 inches) bust, 50.8cm (20 inches) waist and 71cm (28 inches) hip measurement, the centre front is 35.5cm (14 inches) and the centre back is 33cm (13 inches). Each panel is shaped to create the cinched in waist popular during this period.

The corset has a simple construction with fewer panels than most corsets from this period. It has no manufacturer's label and although beautifully constructed it is quite simple and may have been made at home using details obtained from women's magazines and periodicals. The left-hand side of the front opening has an additional wooden piece to add strength at the centre front.

There are boning channels over each seam; these are top stitched onto the top side of the corset. There are also bone channels in the centre of panels two and three. The metal busk at the centre front has five studs and eyelets. The corset is close fitting and although lightly boned would have provided the ability to control and shape the figure.

I have included the 1890 corset pattern for its ability to create an accurate period shape with only eight panels, providing a good generic corset for the mid- to late 19th century. For this pattern I have kept the same number of bone channels as the original corset as it is not heavily boned. I have also followed the top line of the original corset for authenticity; this is level with the bust point. If the corset is being worn without a chemise or camisole you may wish to raise this by approximately 2cm for modesty.

Opposite: 1890 black corset with floral bone channels.

Hereford Museum Resource and Learning Centre, Hereford, England.

Original 1890 black glazed cotton corset pattern

The lines on the 1890 historical corset pattern diagram opposite are a guide for drafting the new pattern onto the female basic block. The approximate position of the **point to point** line, **waist**line and **hip** line are shown on the diagram, it is also labelled with the **CB** and **CF** and lines **C** and **D** which are additional guidelines for the position of **Panel 2** and **Panel 3**.

The front and back views of the original 1890 four panel corset shows the seam lines, bone channels and front busk.

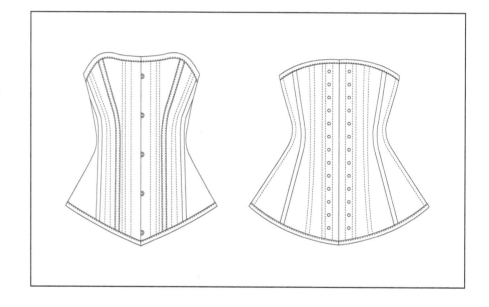

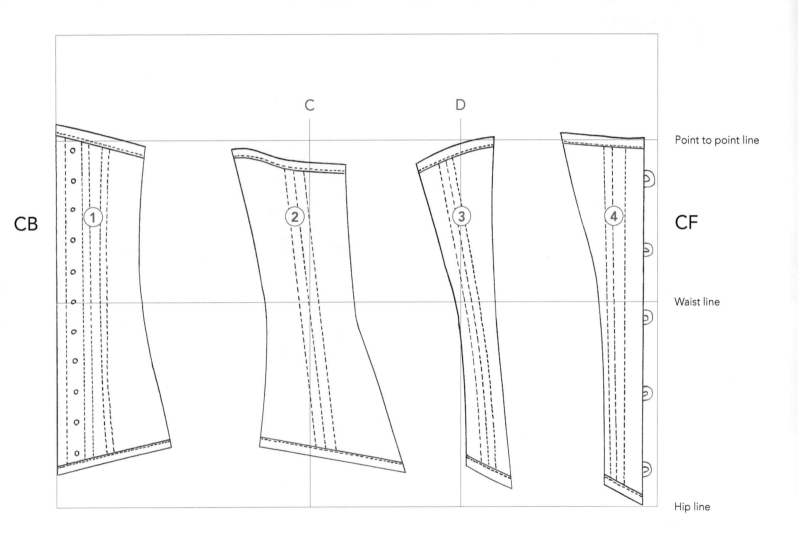

CB

C

D

CF

Point to point line

Waist line

Hip line

1

2

3

4

Guidelines for the 1890 black cotton corset pattern

Trace and separate the female basic block pattern following the instructions in Chapter 5, 'Preparing the female basic block for your historic pattern'. Leave a gap of **30cm** between the basic block back side seam and basic block front side seam and number each line.

Draw in the following additional guidelines

7 to **8**   **point to point** line

The **point to point** line lies at the base of the **bust** dart square across from the **CB** line to the **CF** line

9 to **10**   **mid-hip** line

The **mid-hip** line lies half measurement (**3** to **5**) square across from the **CB** line to the **CF** line

11 to **12** **lower mid-hip** line

The **lower mid-hip** line lies half measurement (**9** to **5**) square across from the **CB** line to the **CF** line

Front detail of the 1890 corset showing the bust panels and applied bone channels.

Hereford Museum Resource and Learning Centre, Hereford, England.

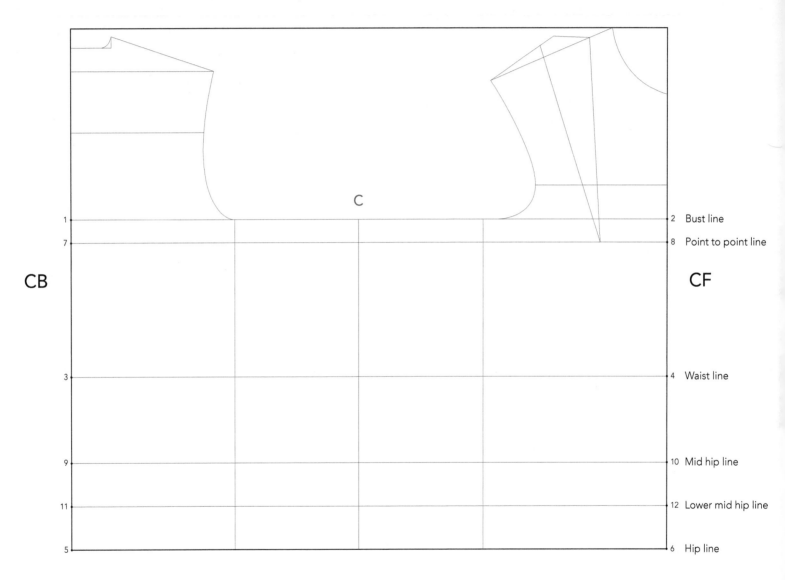

C

CB

CF

1 — 2 Bust line
7 — 8 Point to point line

3 — 4 Waist line

9 — 10 Mid hip line

11 — 12 Lower mid hip line

5 — 6 Hip line

1890 black cotton corset measurement tables

The tables below contain measurements for each pattern piece. Find the **bust**, **waist** and **hip** measurements that are the closest to that of your model. The calculation for the size of each panel is recorded horizontally to these measurements.

1890 black cotton corset measurement table for the bust

Bust measurement	Reduced bust measurement	Half reduced bust measurement	Panel 1	Panel 2	Panel 3	Panel 4
80cm	78cm	39cm	9.5cm	12cm	8.5cm	9cm
82cm	80cm	40cm	9.7cm	12.5cm	8.6cm	9.2cm
86cm	84cm	42cm	10.4cm	13.1cm	9cm	9.5cm
90cm	88cm	44cm	10.8cm	13.7cm	9.5cm	10cm
94cm	92cm	46cm	11.3cm	14.2cm	10cm	10.5cm
100cm	98cm	49cm	12cm	15.2cm	10.6cm	11.2cm
106cm	104cm	52cm	13cm	16cm	11.2cm	11.8cm
112cm	110cm	55cm	14cm	17cm	11.8cm	12.2cm
118cm	116cm	58cm	14.8cm	18.cm	12.4cm	12.8cm
124cm	122cm	61cm	15.5cm	19cm	13.1cm	13.4cm

1890 black cotton corset measurement table for the waist

Full waist measurement	Reduced waist measurement	Half reduced waist measurement	Panel 1	Panel 2	Panel 3	Panel 4
62cm	57cm	28.5cm	9.2cm	10cm	4.5cm	4.8cm
64cm	59cm	29.5cm	9.4cm	10.3cm	4.8cm	5cm
68cm	63cm	31.5cm	10cm	11cm	5.2cm	5.3cm
72cm	67cm	33.5cm	10.4cm	12cm	5.5cm	5.6cm
76cm	71cm	35.5cm	11cm	12.7cm	5.8cm	6cm
82cm	77cm	38.5cm	12cm	13.7cm	6.3cm	6.5cm
88cm	83cm	41.5cm	13cm	14.7cm	6.8cm	7cm
94cm	89cm	44.5cm	14cm	15.8cm	7.2cm	7.5cm
100cm	95cm	47.5cm	15cm	17cm	7.7cm	7.8cm
104cm	99cm	49.5cm	15.7cm	17.8cm	7.8cm	8.2cm

1890 black cotton corset measurement table for the hip

Full hip measurement	Half hip measurement	Panel 1	Panel 2	Panel 3	Panel 4
84cm	42cm	14.2cm	18cm	5cm	4.8cm
88cm	44cm	15cm	18.8cm	5.2cm	5cm
92cm	46cm	15.6cm	19.7cm	5.4cm	5.3cm
96cm	48cm	16.3cm	20.4cm	5.7cm	5.6cm
100cm	50cm	16.7cm	21.2cm	6.1cm	6cm
106cm	53cm	17.7cm	22.4cm	6.5cm	6.4cm
112cm	56cm	18.6cm	23.2cm	7.2cm	7cm
118cm	59cm	19.7cm	24.4cm	7.5cm	7.4cm
124cm	62cm	20.5cm	25.6cm	8cm	7.9cm
130cm	65cm	21.6cm	26.7cm	8.4cm	8.3cm

Create a table of measurements for your model

Create an individual table for your model
to isolate the specific measurements
required to draft your historical pattern.
See example table below.

1890 black cotton corset individual measurement table example

Size	Full measurement	Reduced measurement	Half reduced measurement	Panel 1	Panel 2	Panel 3	Panel 4
Bust	90cm	88cm	44cm	10.8cm	13.7cm	9.5cm	10cm
Waist	68cm	63cm	31.5cm	10cm	11cm	5.2cm	5.3cm
Hip	100cm		50cm	16.7cm	21.2cm	6.1cm	6cm

Begin plotting the 1890 black cotton corset onto your traced basic block pattern

When drafting the **1890** corset pattern the **bust** measurements are plotted onto the **point to point** line and the **hip** measurements are plotted on the **hip** line. When this does not apply it is highlighted within the pattern instructions.

Panel 1

3 to **13**	**waist** measurement
7 to **14**	**bust** measurement
5 to **15**	**hip** measurement
15 to **16**	square up from point **15** with a temporary line to the lower **mid-hip** line to find point **16**
14 to **13**	connect with a temporary straight line
13 to **16**	connect with a very slight convex curve

Panel 4

4 to **17**	**waist** measurement
8 to **18**	**bust** measurement
6 to **19**	**hip** measurement
18 to **17**	connect with a temporary straight line
17 to **19**	connect with a straight line

Panel 2

20 to **21**	**waist** measurement distribute equally either side of line **C**
22 to **23**	**bust** measurement distribute four fifths of the **bust** measurement to the left of line **C** and one fifth of the **bust** measurement to the right of line **C**
24 to **25**	**hip** measurement distribute two fifths of the **hip** measurement to the left of line **C** and three fifths of the **hip** measurement to the right of line **C**
24 to **26**	square up from point **24** with a temporary line to the **lower mid-hip** line to find point **26**
25 to **27**	square up from point **25** with a temporary line to the **lower mid-hip** line to find point **27**
22 to **20**	connect with a temporary straight line
20 to **26**	connect with a very slight convex curve
23 to **21**	connect with a very shallow concave curve
21 to **27**	connect with a temporary straight line

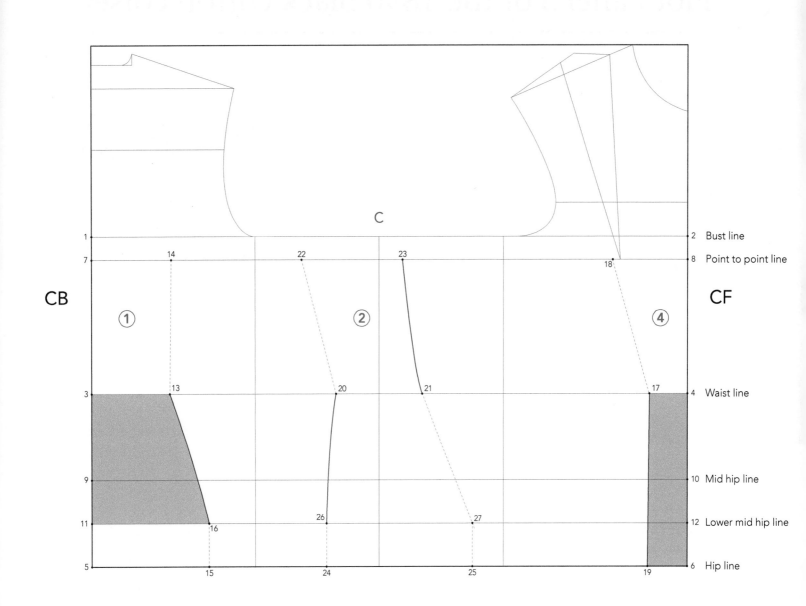

CB

CF

C

① ② ④

2 Bust line
8 Point to point line
4 Waist line
10 Mid hip line
12 Lower mid hip line
6 Hip line

Plot Panel 3 of the 1890 black cotton corset

Draw in the following additional guideline

Line **D**	on the **waist**line mark half measurement (**21** to **17**) square up to **bust** line and down tothe **hip** line

Panel 3

28	lies at the junction of the **waist**line and line **D**
28 to **29**	**waist** measurement to the right of line **D**
30 to **31**	**bust** measurement distribute two fifths of the **bust** measurement to the left of line **D** and three fifths of the **bust** measurement to the right of line **D**
32	lies at the junction of the **hip** line and line **D**
32 to **33**	**0.5cm** to the right of line **D**
33 to **34**	**hip** measurement

30 to **28**	connect with a very shallow concave curve
28 to **33**	connect with a very shallow concave curve
31 to **29**	connect with a temporary straight line
29 to **34**	connect with a straight line

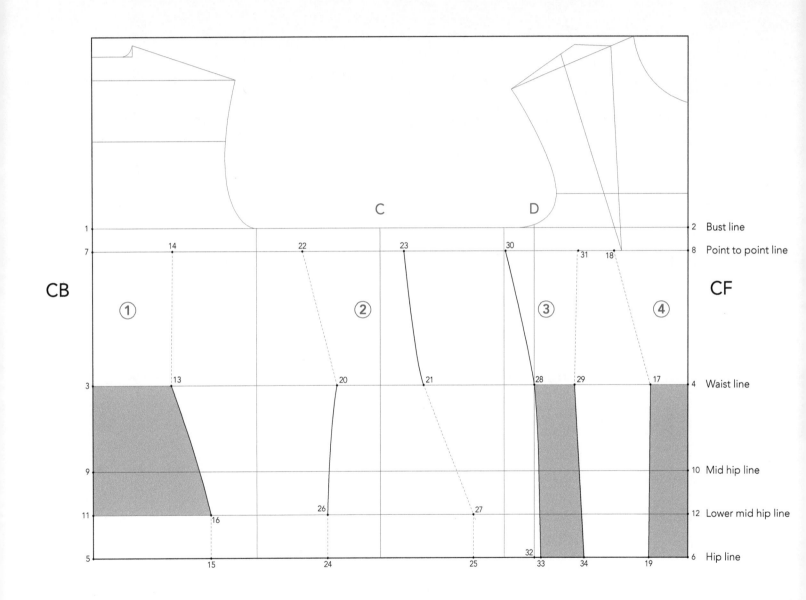

CB

CF

C

D

① ② ③ ④

14 22 23 30 31 18

13 20 21 28 29 17

16 26 27 32

15 24 25 33 34 19

2	Bust line
8	Point to point line
4	Waist line
10	Mid hip line
12	Lower mid hip line
6	Hip line

1
7
3
9
11
5

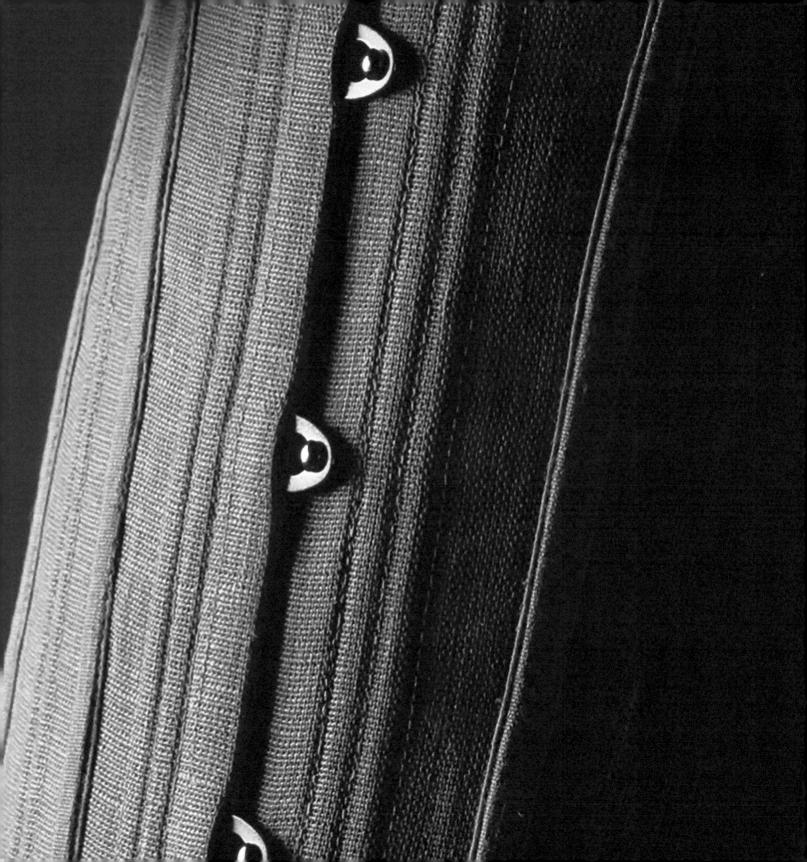

Extend the top of the 1890 black cotton corset pattern

Panel 1

1 to **35**	half measurement (**1** to **7**) on the **CB** line
14 to **36**	**0.6cm** on line (**14** to **13**)
13 to **37**	one third measurement (**13** to **36**)
37 to **38**	square across **0.3cm**

36 through **38** to **13** connect with a very shallow concave curve

Panel 2

Measure temporary line **13** to **36** on **Panel 1** transfer measurement to **Panel 2** from point **20** to find point **39**

20 to **40**	one third measurement (**20** to **39**)
40 to **41**	square across **0.3cm**

20 through **41** to **39** connect with a shallow concave curve

Ensure that line (**20** through **41** to **39**) is the same length as (**13** through **38** to **36**)

23 to **42**   **1.6cm**

Panel 3

Measure line **21** to **42** on **Panel 2** transfer measurement to **Panel 3** from point **28** to find point **43**

31 to **44**	extend line (**29** to **31**) by **0.6cm** to find point **44**
29 to **46**	one third measurement (**29** to **44**)
44 to **47**	one third measurement (**29** to **44**)
46 to **48**	square across **0.3cm**

44 through **47** and **48** to **29** connect with a continuous curve using the diagram as a guide

Panel 4

Measure temporary line **29** through **46**, **31** to **44** on **Panel 3** transfer measurement to **Panel 4** from point **17** through **18** to find point **45** – depending on the size of your corset this point may fall close to point **18**

17 to **49**	one third measurement (**17** to **45**)
45 to **50**	one third measurement (**17** to **45**)
49 to **51**	square across **0.3cm**

45 through **50** and **51** to **17** connect with a continuous curve using the diagram as a guide

Ensure that line (**45** through **50** and **51** to **17**) is the same length as (**44** through **47** and **48** to **29**) – adjust if necessary

8 to **52**   **0.6cm** on **CF** line

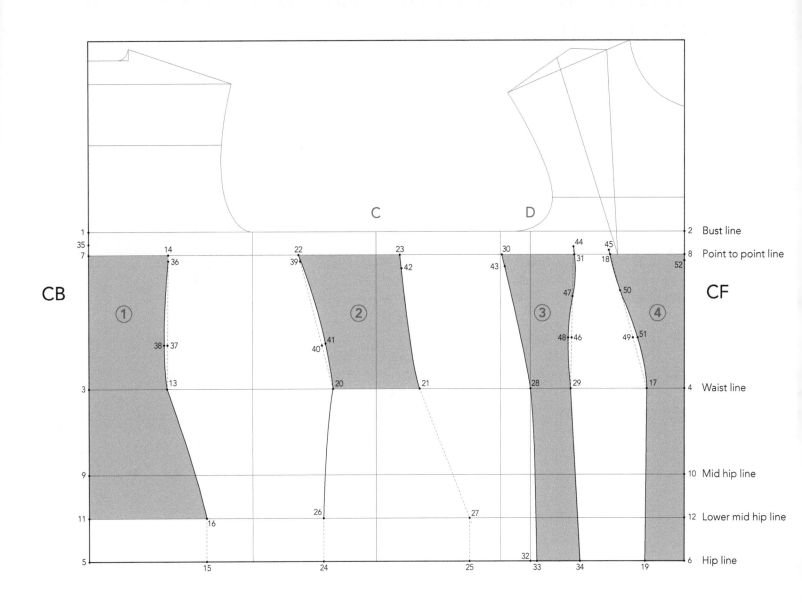

CB

CF

C

D

① ② ③ ④

Bust line
Point to point line
Waist line
Mid hip line
Lower mid hip line
Hip line

Extend the bottom of your 1890 black cotton corset pattern

Panel 1

11 to **53**	half measurement (**11** to **5**) on the **CB** line
16 to **54**	**0.6cm** on line (**13** to **16**)

Panel 2

Measure line **20** to **26** on **Panel 2** ensure that it is the same length as line **13** to **54** on **Panel 1** – adjust if necessary

21 to **55**	extend line (**21** to **27**) by **0.6cm** to find point **55**
21 to **56**	two thirds measurement (**21** to **55**)
56 to **57**	square across **0.2cm**

21 through **57** to **55** connect with a slight convex curve

Panel 3

Measure line **21** through **57** to **55** on **Panel 2** transfer measurement to **Panel 3** from point **28** to find point **58**

59	lies at the junction of line (**29** to **34**) and the lower **mid-hip** line
59 to **60**	two thirds measurement (**59** to **34**)

Panel 4

Measure line **29** through **59** to **60** on **Panel 3** transfer measurement to **Panel 4** from point **17** to find point **61**

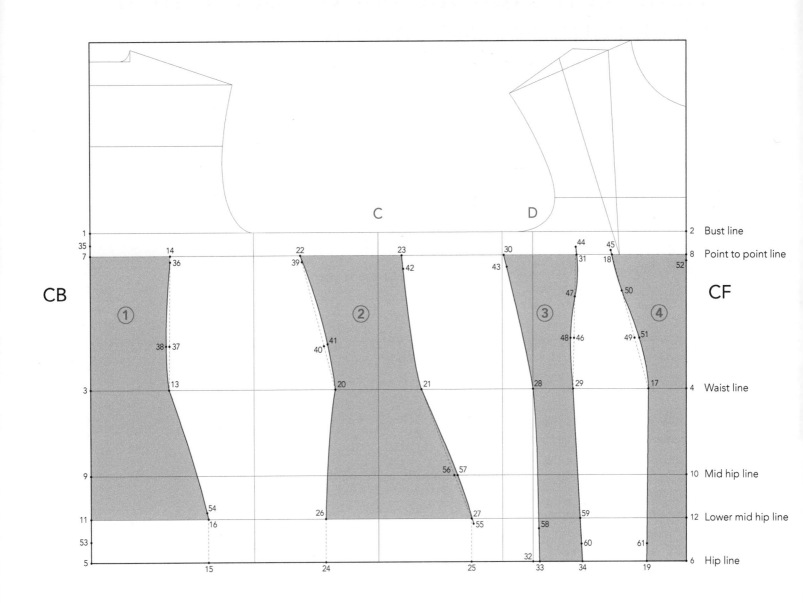

CB

CF

C

D

① ② ③ ④

Bust line

Point to point line

Waist line

Mid hip line

Lower mid hip line

Hip line

Connect the top and bottom of the 1890 black cotton corset pattern

1890 corset top line

Panel 1

35 to **36** connect with a slight convex curve

Panel 2

39 to **42** connect with a temporary straight line

Divide line (**39** to **42**) by **3** to find points **62** and **63**

63 to **64** square down **0.2cm**

39 through **62** and **64** to **42** connect with a continuous curve using the diagram as a guide

Panel 3

43 to **44** connect with a temporary straight line

44 to **65** one third measurement (**43** to **44**)

65 to **66** square up **0.3cm**

43 through **66** to **44** connect with a slight convex curve

Panel 4

45 to **52** connect with a temporary straight line

45 to **67** one third measurement (**45** to **52**)

67 to **68** square up **0.3cm**

45 through **68** to **52** connect with a slight convex curve

1890 Corset Bottom line

Panel 1

53 to **54** connect with a slight convex curve

Panel 2

26 to **55** connect with a very shallow concave curve

Panel 3

58 to **60** connect with a straight line

Panel 4

61 to **6** connect with a slight convex curve

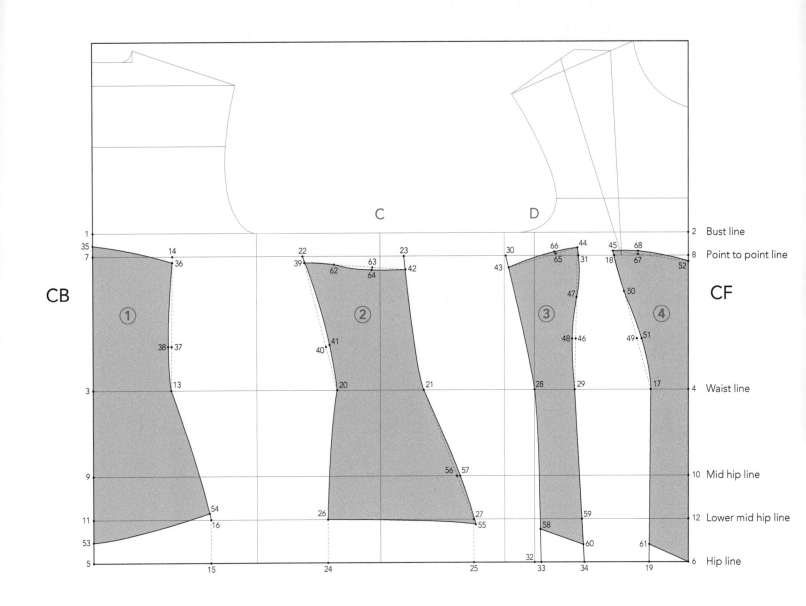

CB

CF

① ② ③ ④

C

D

Bust line
Point to point line
Waist line
Mid hip line
Lower mid hip line
Hip line

Draw the bone channels on your completed 1890 black cotton corset pattern

Use the diagram as a guide when drawing in your bone channels; these are **0.7cm** wide with bones that are **0.5cm** wide. If you wish you can use a **1cm** wide bone channel with a **0.7cm** wide bone. At the centre back there is a central eyelet channel that is **1.3cm** wide on both sides for lacing up the corset. The bone channels on each seam are sewn on the right side of the corset, and a decorative channel is sewn over the trimmed seam; this is optional. A simpler alternative is to sew a fell seam to the right of each seam and use this as a bone channel. The busk channel at the centre front is **1.3cm** wide on each side.

When tracing your pattern, mark the number on each panel and the **waist** position to help you identify them accurately and align each piece when sewing your corset together. Each half of the corset connects in numerical order as they are seen on the pattern.

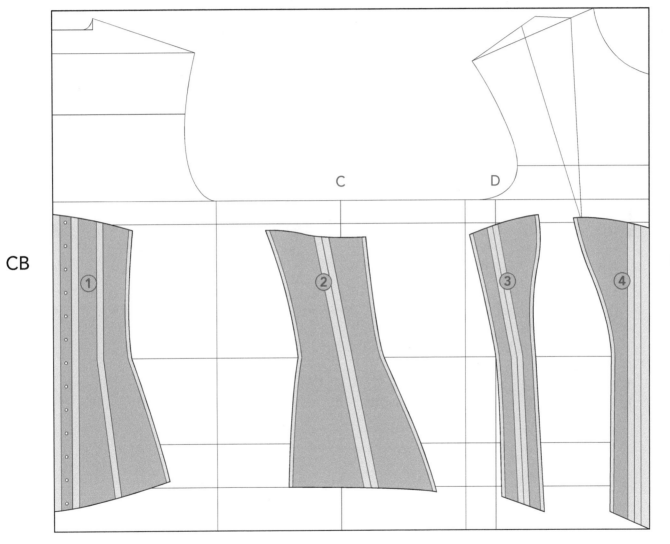

CB

CF

C

D

13 1890 Celebrated
C.B. Bridal Corset

1890 Celebrated C.B. Bridal Corset

The 1890 Celebrated C.B. Bridal Corset is a beautiful example of a manufactured corset produced during the second half of the 19th century, and is part of the costume collection held by Hampshire Museum Services, at Chilcombe House, England. The corset was made by Charles Bayer & Co of London Wall, a manufacturing company established in the late 19th century. Adverts boasted the corsets were made of the finest French fabrics and were easy fitting to render the hourglass figure required by women of the period. The corset has a waist tape that is stamped "Celebrated C.B. Bridal Corset, none genuine unless stamped with the trademark C.B. Corsets Rd." It was available to buy with a straight or spoon busk. The example at Hampshire Museum services has a spoon busk.

Opposite: 1890 Celebrated C.B. Bridal Corset made from ivory satin.

From the collections of Hampshire Cultural Trust.

The Celebrated C.B. Bridal Corset is made from ivory silk satin backed on cotton coutil and has a deep 8.9cm (3.5 inches) wide lace trim with ribbon insert around the top edge; this stands proud by 2.5cm (1 inch) for modesty. The corset is also decorated with delicate flowers in ivory over the bust panels and floss embroidery at the top and bottom of each bone channel. The corset is in excellent condition, with the original silk ribbon for lacing the corset remaining. Inside the left bust some loose threads remain that may have attached some additional padding; this is not with the garment.

The corset has twelve panels; the seams are hidden under an applied three bone wide bone channel that is top stitched onto the right side of the corset. At the front the applied bone channels over the bust seam give the effect of bust gussets and provides space for the floral decoration. The centre front is 34.5cm (13.5 inches) long and has a spoon busk. The centre back is 33cm (13 inches) long. It is laced, with 18 black metal eyelets on each side.

This 1890 corset has a waist measurement of 53.5cm (21 inches) and bust and hip measurements of 91.5cm (36 inches). The corset is machine stitched throughout and has probably been steam moulded during the manufacturing process. From 1880 onwards steam moulding was used to give corsets their final shape, wet starch was applied to the garment and was heated and then cooled on a specially shaped female block. This along with the thirty six whalebones produced an extremely rigid final corset.

The Celebrated C.B. Bridal Corset pattern is relatively straightforward as the panels are mainly vertical. I have included the same bone channels as the original on the final pattern, although this could be simplified by replacing the multiple bone channels with one on each seam. Examples of the 1890 corset with the applied bone channels and with a single bone channel in each seam are shown in the photographs throughout the instructions. The original top line of the corset is level with the bust point; you may wish to raise this by approximately 2cm for modesty.

Original 1890 Celebrated C.B. Bridal Corset pattern

The lines on the 1890 historical corset pattern diagram opposite are a guide for drafting the new pattern onto the female basic block. The approximate position of the **bust** line, **waist**line and **hip** line are shown on the diagram. It is also labelled with the **CB** and **CF** and lines **B**, **C**, **D** and **F**, which are additional guidelines for the position of **Panel 2**, **Panel 3**, **Panel 4** and **Panel 5**.

The front and back views of the original 1890 Celebrated C.B. Bridal Corset Pattern shows the seam lines, applied boning channels and spoon busk.

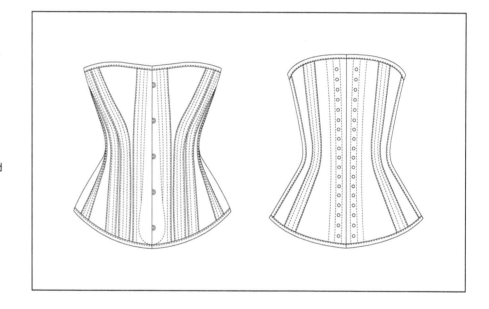

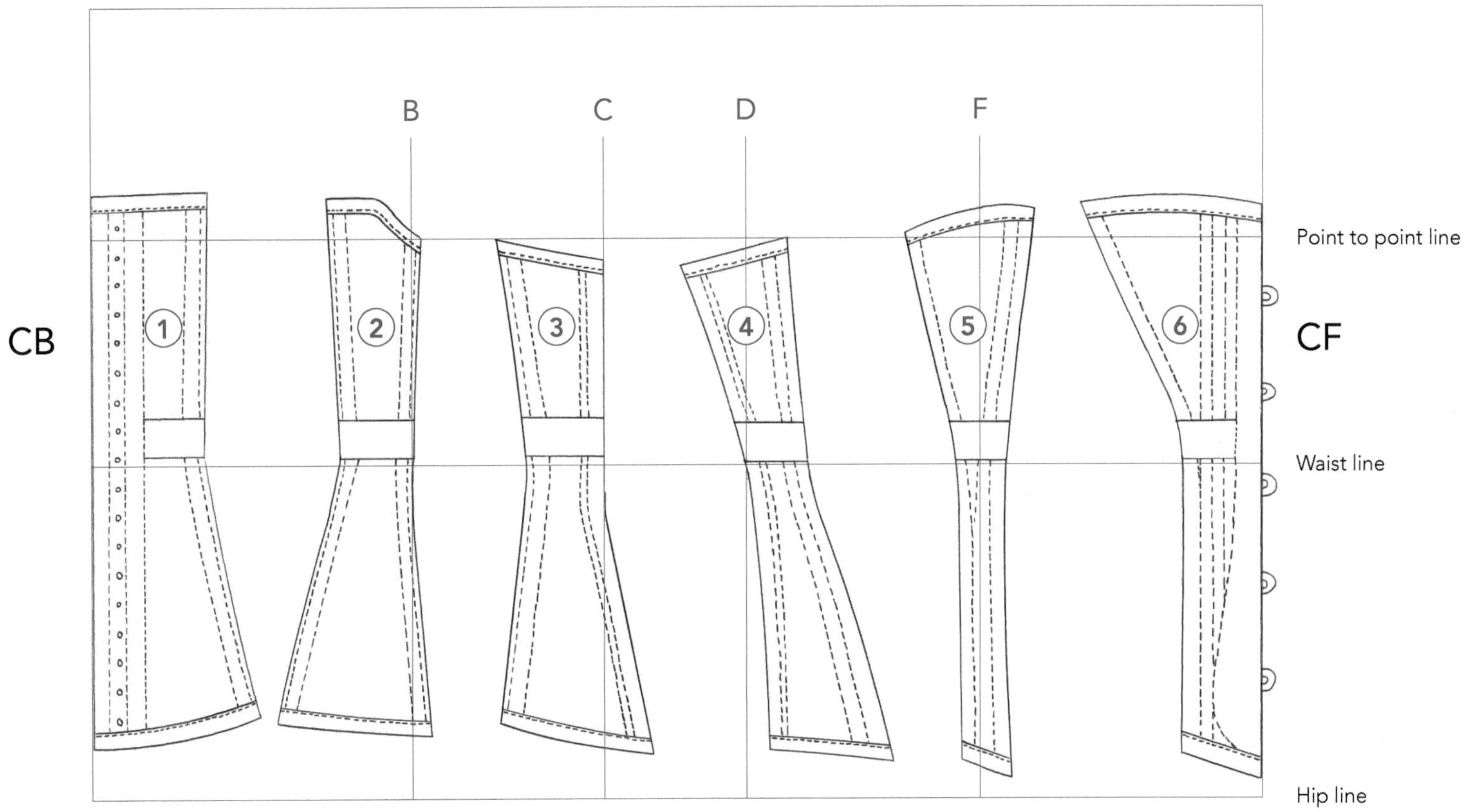

CB

B   C   D   F

① ② ③ ④ ⑤ ⑥

CF

Point to point line

Waist line

Hip line

Guidelines for the 1890 Celebrated C.B. Bridal Corset pattern

Trace and separate the female basic block pattern following the instructions in Chapter 5, 'Preparing the female basic block for your historic pattern'. Leave a gap of **30cm** between the basic block back side seam and basic block front side seam and number each line.

Draw in the following additional guidelines

7 to **8   point to point** line

The **point to point** line lies at the base of the **bust** dart square across from the **CB** line to the **CF** line

9 to **10 mid-hip** line

The **mid-hip** line lies half measurement (**3** to **5**) square across from the **CB** line to the **CF** line

11 to **12 lower mid-hip** line

The **lower mid-hip** line lies half measurement (**9** to **5**) square across from the **CB** line to the **CF** line

Line **B**   mark your traced female basic block back side seam line **B**

Line **E**   mark your traced female basic block front side seam line **E**

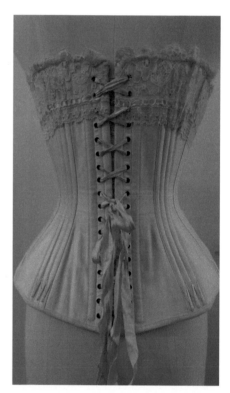

1890 Celebrated C.B. Bridal Corset back view and front detail showing the bust panels and applied lace. From the collections of Hampshire Cultural Trust.

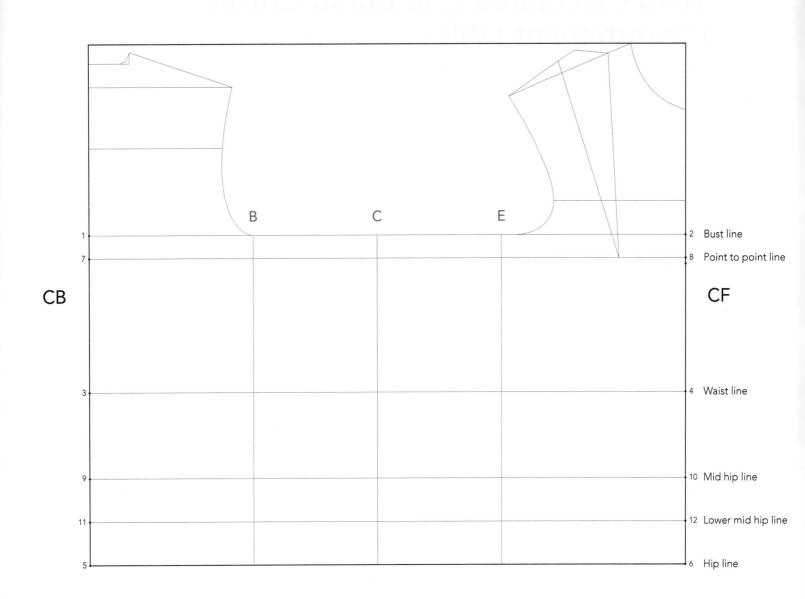

CB   CF

B	C	E

1 ————— 2 Bust line

7 ————— 8 Point to point line

3 ————— 4 Waist line

9 ————— 10 Mid hip line

11 ————— 12 Lower mid hip line

5 ————— 6 Hip line

1890 Celebrated C.B. Bridal Corset measurement tables

The tables below contain measurements for each pattern piece. Find the **bust**, **waist** and **hip** measurements that are the closest to that of your model. The calculation for the size of each panel is recorded horizontally to these measurements.

1890 Celebrated C.B. Bridal Corset measurement table for the bust

Bust measurement	Reduced bust measurement	Half reduced bust measurement	Panel 1	Panel 2	Panel 3	Panel 4	Panel 5	Panel 6
80cm	78cm	39cm	6.8cm	6cm	5.4cm	5.4cm	6.6cm	8.8cm
82cm	80cm	40cm	7cm	6cm	5.6cm	5.6cm	6.8cm	9cm
86cm	84cm	42cm	7.2cm	6.2cm	6cm	6cm	7.2cm	9.4cm
90cm	88cm	44cm	7.4cm	6.8cm	6.3cm	6.3cm	7.5cm	9.7cm
94cm	92cm	46cm	7.8cm	7cm	6.6cm	6.6cm	7.8cm	10.2cm
100cm	98cm	49cm	8.8cm	7.4cm	7cm	7cm	8cm	10.8cm
106cm	104cm	52cm	9.8cm	8cm	7.4cm	7.4cm	8.4cm	11cm
112cm	110cm	55cm	10.6cm	8.6cm	7.7cm	7.7cm	8.8cm	11.6cm
118cm	116cm	58cm	11.2cm	9cm	8.3cm	8.3cm	9.2cm	12cm
124cm	122cm	61cm	11.5cm	9.4cm	8.7cm	8.7cm	10cm	12.7cm

1890 Celebrated C.B. Bridal Corset measurement table for the waist

Full waist measurement	Reduced waist measurement	Half reduced waist measurement	Panel 1	Panel 2	Panel 3	Panel 4	Panel 5	Panel 6
62cm	57cm	28.5cm	6.8cm	4.7cm	4.7cm	4.2cm	3.1cm	5cm
64cm	59cm	29.5cm	7cm	4.8cm	4.8cm	4.5cm	3.2cm	5.2cm
68cm	63cm	31.5cm	7.2cm	5.2cm	5.2cm	4.9cm	3.6cm	5.4cm
72cm	67cm	33.5cm	7.4cm	5.6cm	5.6cm	5.4cm	3.8cm	5.7cm
76cm	71cm	35.5cm	7.8cm	6cm	6cm	5.6cm	4.1cm	6cm
82cm	77cm	38.5cm	8.8cm	6.5cm	6.5cm	6cm	4.5cm	6.2cm
88cm	83cm	41.5cm	9.8cm	7cm	7cm	6.3cm	5cm	6.4cm
94cm	89cm	44.5cm	10.6cm	7.6cm	7.6cm	6.6cm	5.5cm	6.6cm
100cm	95cm	47.5cm	11.5cm	8.2cm	8.2cm	7cm	5.8cm	6.8cm
104cm	99cm	49.5cm	11.8cm	8.5cm	8.5cm	7.5cm	6.2cm	7cm

1890 Celebrated C.B. Bridal Corset measurement table for the hips

Full hip measurement	Reduced hip measurement	Half reduced hip measurement	Panel 1	Panel 2	Panel 3	Panel 4	Panel 5	Panel 6
84cm	82cm	41cm	9.3cm	8.8cm	8.5cm	6.5cm	3cm	4.9cm
88cm	86cm	43cm	9.6cm	9.3cm	8.7cm	7cm	3.2cm	5.2cm
92cm	90cm	45cm	10cm	9.6cm	9.3cm	7.3cm	3.5cm	5.4cm
96cm	94cm	47cm	10.4cm	10cm	9.6cm	7.6cm	3.8cm	5.6cm
100cm	98cm	49cm	10.9cm	10.4cm	10cm	8cm	4.1cm	5.8cm
106cm	104cm	52cm	11.5cm	11cm	10.5cm	8.5cm	4.5cm	6cm
112cm	110cm	55cm	12cm	11.8cm	11.2cm	9cm	4.8cm	6.2cm
118cm	116cm	58cm	12.7cm	12.3cm	12cm	9.4cm	5.4cm	6.4cm
124cm	122cm	61cm	13.6cm	12.8cm	12.5cm	10cm	5.5cm	6.6cm
130cm	128cm	64cm	14.5cm	13.4cm	13cm	10.5cm	5.8cm	6.8cm

Create a table of measurements for your model

Create an individual table for your model to isolate the specific measurements required to draft your historical pattern. See example table below.

1890 Celebrated C.B. Bridal Corset individual measurement table example

Size	Full measurement	Reduced measurement	Half reduced measurement	Panel 1	Panel 2	Panel 3	Panel 4	Panel 5	Panel 6
Bust	90cm	88cm	44cm	7.4cm	6.8cm	6.3cm	6.3cm	7.5cm	9.7cm
Waist	68cm	63cm	31.5cm	7.2cm	5.2cm	5.2cm	4.9cm	3.6cm	5.4cm
Hip	100cm	98cm	49cm	10.8cm	10.3cm	10cm	8cm	4.1cm	5.8cm

Begin plotting the 1890 Celebrated C.B. Bridal Corset onto your traced basic block pattern

When drafting the **1890** corset pattern the **bust** measurements are plotted onto the **point to point** line and the **hip** measurements are plotted onto the **lower mid-hip** line. When this does not apply it is highlighted within the pattern instructions.

Panel 1

3 to **13**	**waist** measurement
7 to **14**	**bust** measurement
11 to **15**	**hip** measurement
14 to **13**	connect with a straight line
13 to **15**	connect with a straight line

Panel 6

4 to **16**	**waist** measurement
8 to **17**	**bust** measurement
12 to **18**	**hip** measurement
17 to **16**	connect with a temporary straight line
16 to **18**	connect with a straight line

Panel 3

19	lies at the junction of the **waist**line and line **C**
19 to **20**	**waist** measurement to the left of line **C**
21	lies at the junction of the **point** to **point** line and line **C**
21 to **22**	**0.6cm** to the left of line **C**
22 to **23**	**bust** measurement
24 to **25**	**hip** measurement distribute two thirds **hip** measurement to the left of line **C** and one third **hip** measurement to the right of line **C**
23 to **20**	connect with a straight line
20 to **24**	connect with a straight line
22 to **19**	connect with a straight line
19 to **25**	connect with a temporary straight line

Panel 2

26	lies at the junction of the **waist**line and line **B**
26 to **27**	**waist** measurement to left of line **B**
28	lies at the junction of the **point** to **point** line and line **B**
28 to **29**	**0.6cm** to the right of line **B**
29 to **30**	**bust** measurement
31 to **32**	**hip** measurement distribute five sixths **hip** measurement to the left of line **B** and one sixth **hip** measurement to the right of line **B**
30 to **27**	connect with a straight line
27 to **31**	connect with a straight line
29 to **26**	connect with a straight line
26 to **32**	connect with a straight line

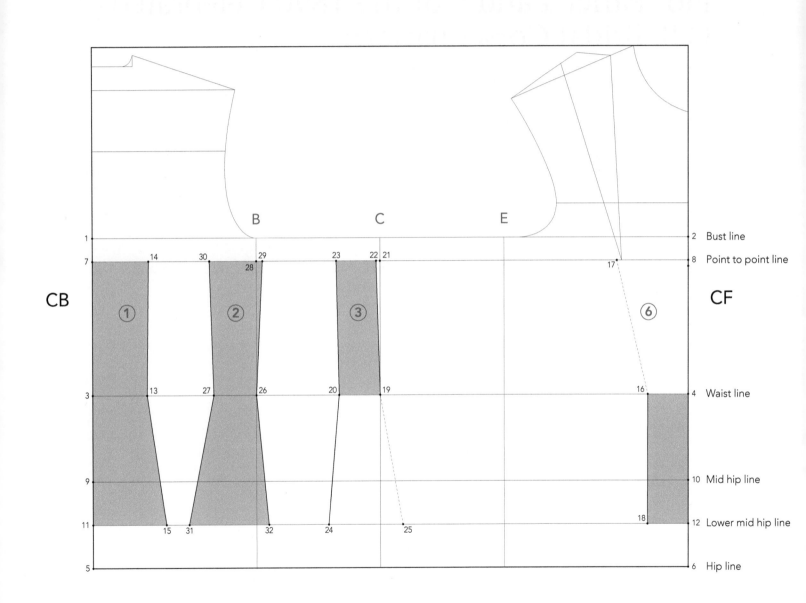

CB

CF

B   C   E

1   2   Bust line

7   8   Point to point line

①   ②   ③   ⑥

14   30   29   28   23   22   21   17

3   4   Waist line

13   27   26   20   19   16

9   10   Mid hip line

11   12   Lower mid hip line

15   31   32   24   25   18

5   6   Hip line

Plot Panel 4 and 5 of the 1890 Celebrated C.B. Bridal Corset pattern

Draw in the following additional guidelines

Line **D**   on the **waist**line mark half measurement between line **C** and line **E** square up to **bust**line and down to the **hip** line

Line **F**   on the **waist**line mark one third measurement between line **E** and the **CF** line square up to **bust** line and down to the **hip** line

Panel 4

33   lies at the junction of the **waist**line and line **D**

33 to 34   **waist** measurement to the right of line **D**

35 to 36   **bust** measurement distribute equally either side of line **D**

37   lies at the junction of the **lower mid-hip** line and line **D**

37 to 38   **hip** measurement to the right of line **D**

35 to 33   connect with a straight line

33 to 37   lies on line **D**

36 to 34   connect with a temporary straight line

34 to 38   connect with a straight line

Panel 5

39 to 40   **waist** measurement distribute equally either side of line **F**

41 to 42   **bust** measurement distribute half **bust** measurement plus **0.5cm** to the left of line **F** and half **bust** measurement minus **0.5cm** to the right of line **F**

43 to 44   **hip** measurement distribute equally either side of line **F**

41 to 39   connect with a temporary straight line

39 to 43   connect with a straight line

42 to 40   connect with a temporary straight line

40 to 44   connect with a straight line

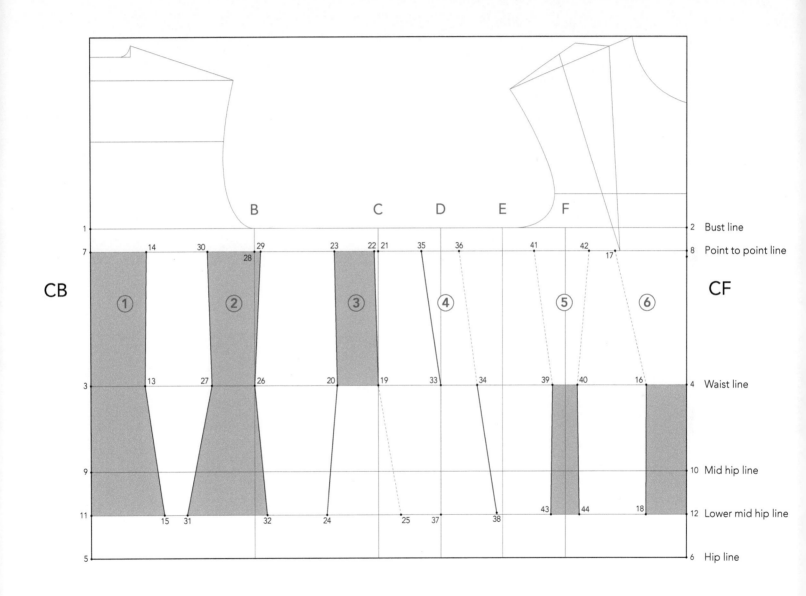

CB

CF

B   C   D   E   F

① ② ③ ④ ⑤ ⑥

2   Bust line
8   Point to point line
4   Waist line
10   Mid hip line
12   Lower mid hip line
6   Hip line

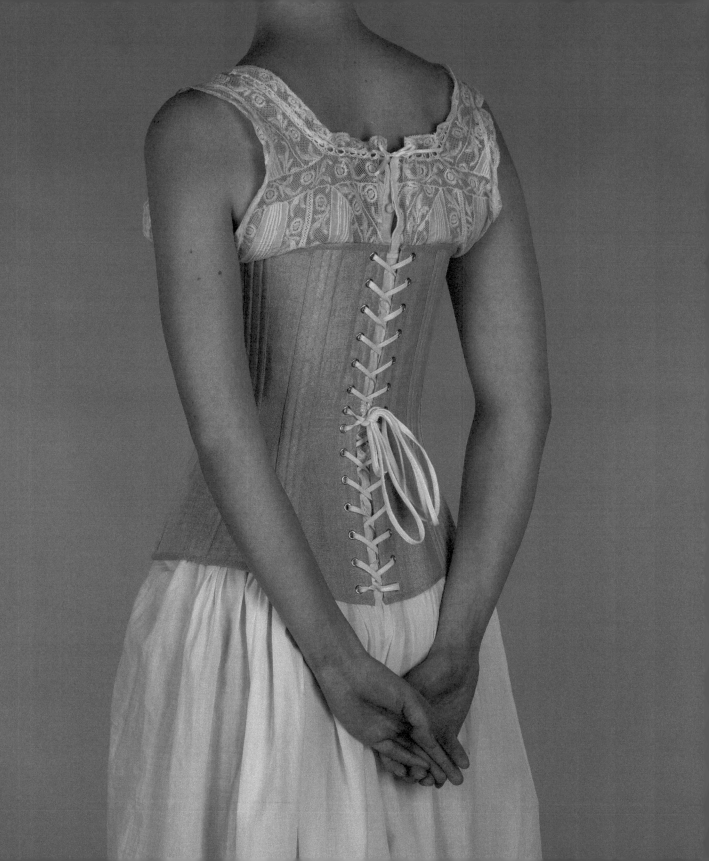

Shape the top of the 1890 Celebrated C.B. Bridal Corset pattern

Panel 1

1 to 45   1.5cm on the **CB** line

14 to 46   extend line (**13** to **14**) by **2cm** to find point **46**

Panel 2

Measure line **13** through **14** to **46** on **Panel 1** transfer measurement to **Panel 2** from point **27** through **30** to find point **47**

Panel 3

22 to 48   0.7cm

Panel 4

Measure line **19** to **48** on **Panel 3** transfer measurement to **Panel 4** from point **33** to find point **49**

34 to 50   half measurement (**34** to **36**)

50 to 51   square across **0.3cm**

36 through **51** to **34** connect with a shallow concave curve using the diagram as a guide

Panel 5

Measure temporary line **34** to **36** on **Panel 4** transfer measurement to **Panel 5** from point **39** to find point **52** – this may be close to point **41**

39 to 53   half measurement (**39** to **52**)

53 to 54   square across **0.3cm**

52 through **54** to **39** connect with a shallow concave curve using the diagram as a guide.

Ensure that line (**52** through **54** to **39**) is the same length as (**36** through **51** to **34**) – adjust if necessary

42 to 55   extend temporary line (**40** to **42**) to half measurement (**2** to **8**)

40 to 56   one third measurement (**40** to **55**)

40 to 57   half measurement (**40** to **56**)

57 to 58   square across **0.2cm**

55 to 59   half measurement (**55** to **56**)

59 to 60   square across **0.3cm**

55 through **60, 56** and **58** to **40** connect with a continuous curve using the diagram as a guide

Panel 6

Measure temporary line **40** through **42** to **55** on **Panel 5** transfer measurement to **Panel 6** from point **16** through **17** to find point **61**

16 to 62   one third measurement (**16** to **61**)

16 to 63   half measurement (**16** to **62**)

63 to 64   square across **0.2cm**

61 to 65   half measurement (**61** to **62**)

65 to 66   square across **0.3cm**

61 through **66, 62** and **64** to **16** connect with a continuous curve using the diagram as a guide

Ensure that line (**61** through **66, 62** and **64** to **16**) is the same length as (**55** through **60, 56,** and **58** to **40**) adjust if necessary

8 to 67   0.5cm on **CF** line

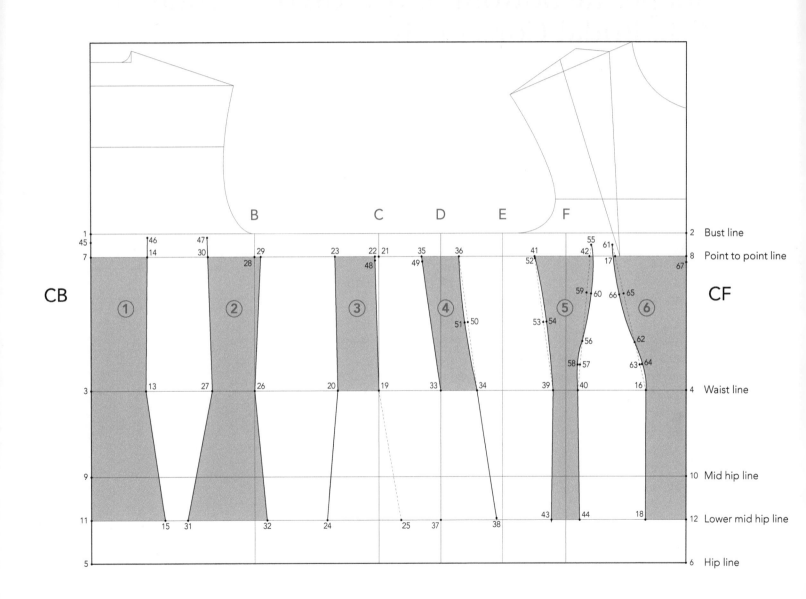

Shape the bottom of the 1890 Celebrated C.B. Bridal Corset pattern

Panel 1

15 to **68** 1cm

Panel 2

Measure line **13** to **68** on **Panel 1** transfer measurement to **Panel 2** from point **27** to find point **69**

32 to **70**   half measurement (**9** to **11**)

Panel 3

Measure line **26** to **70** on **Panel 2** transfer measurement to **Panel 3** from point **20** to find point **71**

25 to **72**   1.3cm
72 to **73**   two thirds measurement (**19** to **72**)
73 to **74**   square across **0.3cm**

19 through **74** to **72** connect with a slight convex curve using the diagram as a guide

Panel 4

Measure temporary line **19** to **72** on **Panel 3** transfer measurement to **Panel 4** from point **33** to find point **75**

75 to **76**   two thirds measurement (**33** to **75**)
76 to **77**   square across **0.3cm**

33 through **77** to **75** connect with a slight convex curve using the diagram as a guide.

Ensure that line (**33** through **77** to **75**) is the same length as (**19** through **74** to **72**) – adjust if necessary

Panel 5

Measure line **34** to **38** on **Panel 4** transfer measurement to **Panel 5** from point **39** to find point **78**– this may be very close to point **43**

44 to **79**   extend line (**40** to **44**) by one third measurement (**12** to **6**) on **CF** line to find point **79**

Panel 6

Measure line **40** through **44** to **79** on **Panel 5** transfer measurement to **Panel 6** from point **16** through **18** to find point **80**

6 to **81**   one third measurement (**12** to **6**) on **CF** line

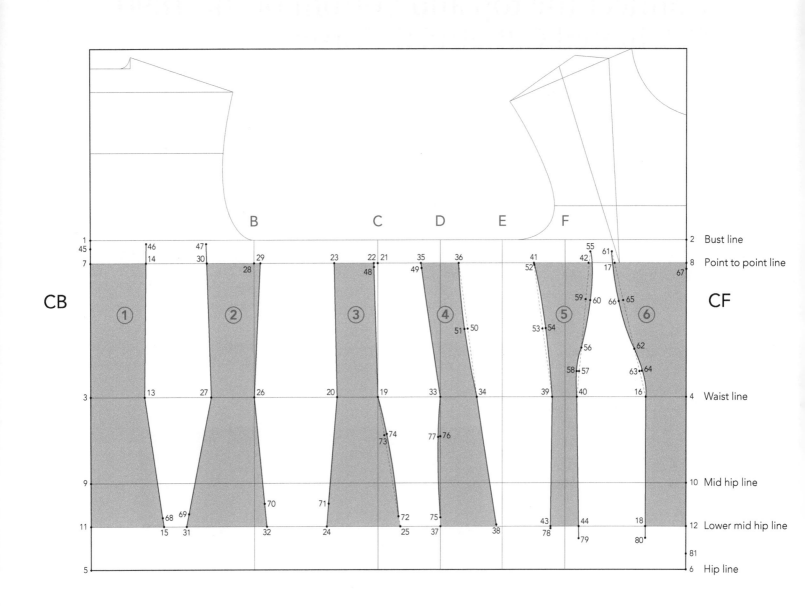

Connect the top and bottom of the 1890 Celebrated C.B. Bridal Corset

1890 corset top line

Panel 1

45 to **46**   connect with a very slight convex curve

Panel 2

47 to **29**   connect with a temporary straight line

47 to **82**   half measurement (**47** to **29**)

82 to **83**   square up **0.7cm**

47 through **83** to **29** connect with a continuous curve using the diagram as a guide

Panel 3

23 to **48**   connect with a straight line

Panel 4

49 to **36**   connect with a very slight convex curve

Panel 5

52 to **55**   connect with a slight convex curve

Panel 6

61 to **67**   connect with a slight convex curve

1890 corset bottom line

Panel 1

11 to **68**   connect with a slight convex curve

Panel 2

69 to **70**   connect with a slight convex curve

Panel 3

71 to **72**   connect with a straight line

Panel 4

75 to **38**   connect with a very shallow concave curve

Panel 5

78 to **79**   connect with a straight line

Panel 6

80 to **81**   connect with a slight convex curve

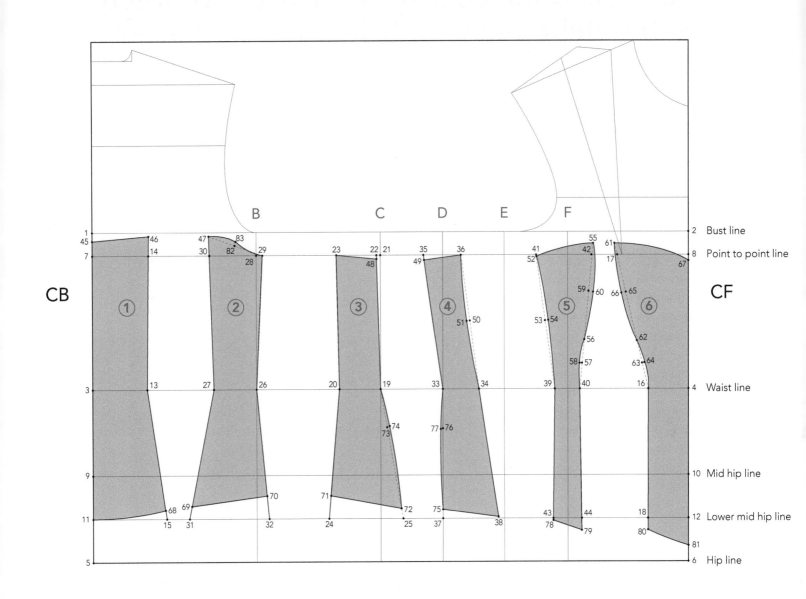

Draw the bone channels on your completed 1890 Celebrated C.B. Bridal Corset pattern

Use the diagram as a guide for the position of your bone channels, these are **0.7cm** wide with bones that are **0.5cm** wide. There are three bone channels across each seam and these are sewn on to the right side of the corset. For a simpler version of this corset the multiple bones channels can be replaced with a **1cm** wide bone channel in each panel seam with **0.7cm** wide bone. The number of bones you include can be adjusted if you require more support; these can be added in the centre of panels 2, 3 and 4. At the centre back there is a central eyelet channel that is **1.3cm** wide on both sides for lacing up the corset. The busk channel at the centre front is shaped to fit a spoon busk; this can be replaced with a straight busk that is **1.3cm** wide on each side.

When tracing your pattern mark the number on each panel and the **waist** position to help you identify them accurately and align each piece when sewing your corset together. Each half of the corset connects in numerical order as they are seen on the pattern.

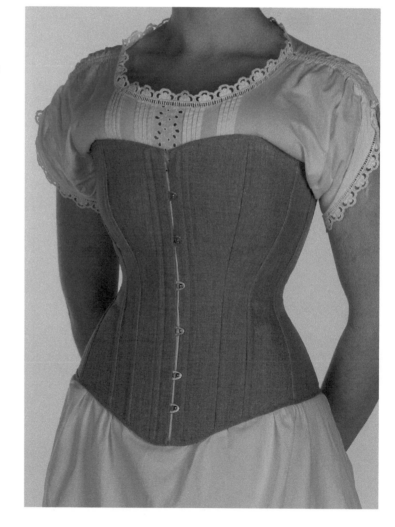

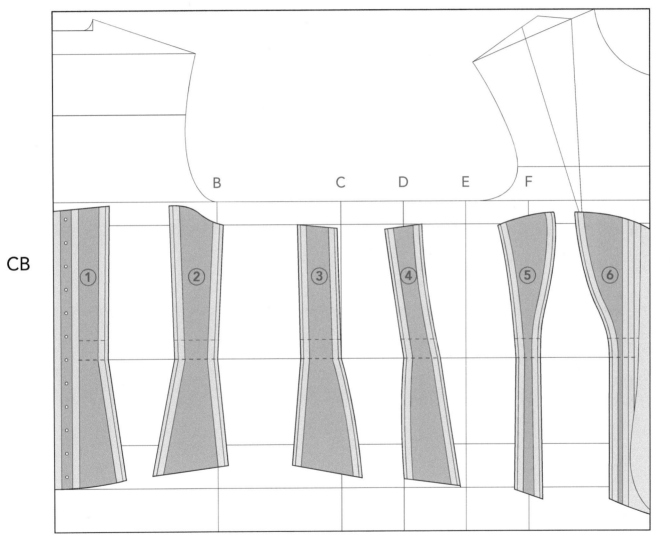

CB

CF

B   C   D   E   F

14 1905 plunge front corset

1905 plunge front corset

The 1905 plunge front corset is held by Leicestershire County Museum services and forms part of the Symington collection. The corset was designed and made in France, the waist tape is printed with "Corset de Paris. Sanakor, Brevete S.G.D.G. France and Belgique. D.R Patent. Patent applied for in England and USA". The patent application was applied for in 1902. The corset is made from black sateen lined with white cotton twill, the top edge is decorated with a narrow black lace and the deep plunge front is tied with a wide ribbon. The front has frilled suspenders with metal slide adjusters. There is a brass loop at the front that was used to hold the folds of a petticoat if it needed to be shorter. The corset is made from 8 panels and is stiffened with whalebone and steel. The corset has an approximate bust measurement of 90cm (35.5 inches), a 56cm (22 inches) waist and mid-hip measurement of 90cm (35.5 inches).

The unique design of this corset produces a beautiful shape that nips the wearer in at the waist, scoops up and over the hips and dips low at the front. The effect is to push the bust up to create the fashionable full breast and low neckline of the early 20th century. The short busk begins between the base of the bust and the waist, allowing the chest to expand whilst giving ample support for the bust. The busk is 25.5cm (10 inches) long with stud and hook fastenings and is lined in black velvet. The centre back is also short 24.5cm (9.5 inches) long and has 13 eyelets on each side. A waist tape is applied to the corset to reinforce the waist and prevent the stitching on each seam from breaking; this is where the corset is under greatest stress.

The 1905 plunge front corset is a particular favourite of mine as it produces such a wonderful silhouette. For this pattern I have kept the same number of bone channels as the original corset, but have replaced the central wide bone in panel 2 with two narrow bones as these are easier to source. The corset was designed to be worn with a camisole or chemise and without any undergarment is very low over the bust and at the deep V front. You may wish to raise the top of the corset by approximately 2cm for modesty; by leaving a generous seam allowance this can be done at the fitting stage.

Opposite: 1905 plunge front corset.

From the collections of Leicestershire County Council: Symington Collection, England.

Original 1905 plunge front corset pattern

The lines on the 1905 historical corset pattern diagram opposite are a guide for drafting the new pattern onto the female basic block. The approximate position of the **point to point** line, **waist**line and **hip** line are shown on the diagram, it is also labelled with the **CB** and **CF** and lines **C** and **D** which are additional guidelines for the position of **Panel 2** and **Panel 3**.

The front and back views of the original 1890 four panel corset shows the seam lines, bone channels and front busk.

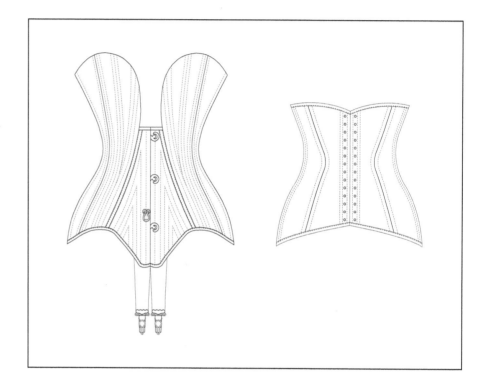

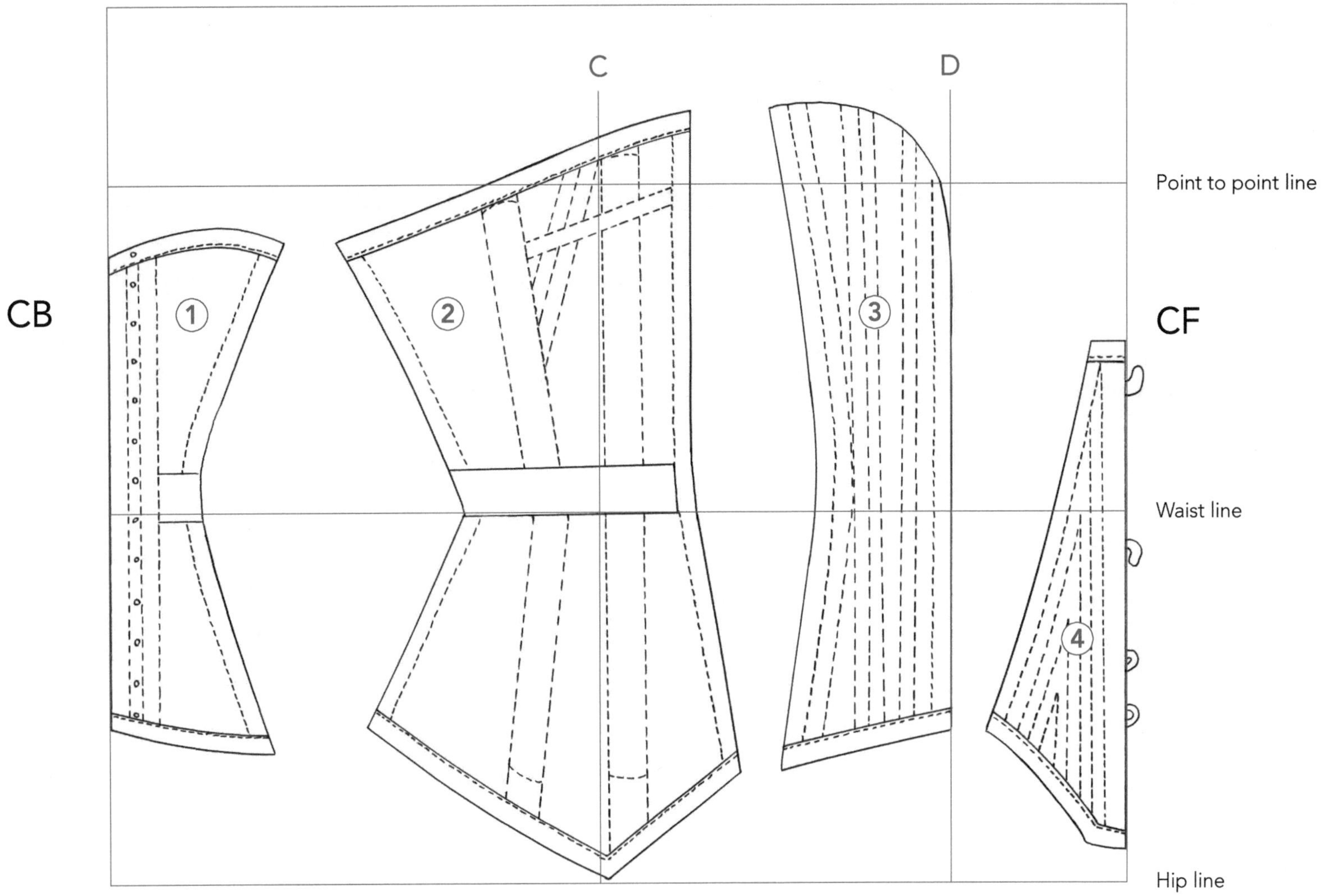

CB

C

D

Point to point line

CF

Waist line

Hip line

① ② ③ ④

Guidelines for the 1905 plunge front corset pattern

Trace and separate the female basic block pattern following the instructions in Chapter 5, 'Preparing the female basic block for your historic pattern'. Leave a gap of **30cm** between the basic block back side seam and basic block front side seam and number each line.

Draw in the following additional guidelines

7 to **8**   **point to point** line

The **point to point** line lies at the base of the **bust** dart square across from the **CB** line to the **CF** line

9 to **10**   **mid-hip** line

The **mid-hip** line lies half measurement (**3** to **5**) square across from the **CB** line to the **CF** line

11 to **12**   **lower mid-hip** line

The **lower mid-hip** line lies half measurement (**9** to **5**) square across from the **CB** line to the **CF** line

Line **D**   draw a line directly down from the bottom of the **bust** dart

Inside detail of the 1905 plunge front corset and garter clasps.

From the collections of Leicestershire County Council: Symington Collection, England.

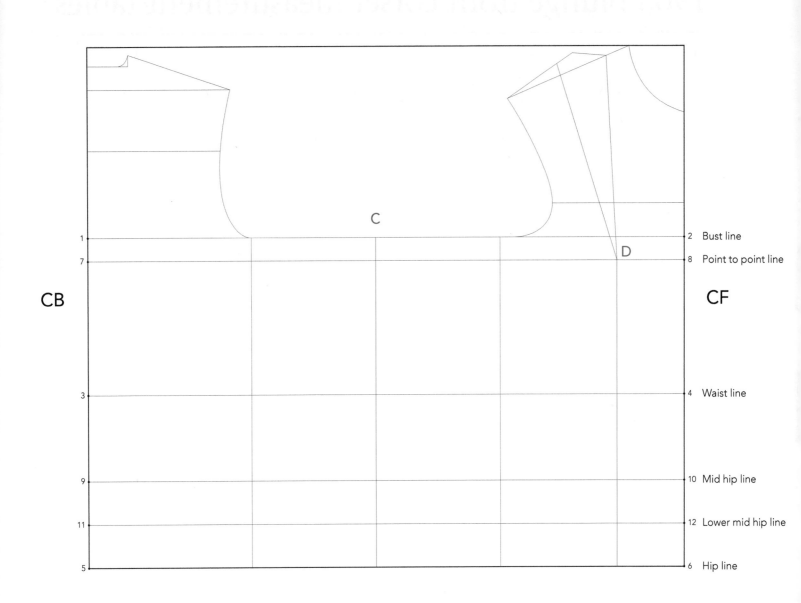

CB

CF

C

D

1   2   Bust line

7   8   Point to point line

3   4   Waist line

9   10   Mid hip line

11   12   Lower mid hip line

5   6   Hip line

1905 plunge front corset measurement tables

The tables below contain measurements for each pattern piece. Find the **bust**, **waist** and **hip** measurements that are the closest to that of your model. The calculation for the size of each panel is recorded horizontally to these measurements.

1905 plunge front corset measurement table for the bust

Bust measurement	Reduced bust measurement	Half reduced bust measurement minus front gap	Panel 1	Panel 2	Panel 3	Panel 4 No measurement
80cm	78cm	37cm	9.5cm	18.8cm	8.7cm	
82cm	80cm	38cm	9.7cm	19.4cm	8.9cm	
86cm	84cm	40cm	10.2cm	20.4cm	9.4cm	
90cm	88cm	42cm	10.8cm	21.4cm	9.8cm	
94cm	92cm	44cm	11.3cm	22.4cm	10.3cm	
100cm	98cm	47cm	12cm	24cm	11cm	
106cm	104cm	50cm	12.8cm	25.5cm	11.7cm	
112cm	110cm	53cm	13.6cm	27cm	12.4cm	
118cm	116cm	56cm	14.4cm	28.4cm	13.2cm	
124cm	122cm	59cm	15cm	30cm	14cm	

1905 plunge front corset measurement table for the waist

Full waist measurement	Reduced waist measurement	Half reduced waist measurement	Panel 1	Panel 2	Panel 3	Panel 4
62cm	57cm	28.5cm	5cm	12.5cm	7.5cm	3.5cm
64cm	59cm	29.5cm	5.2cm	12.9cm	7.7cm	3.7cm
68cm	63cm	31.5cm	5.5cm	13.8cm	8.3cm	3.9cm
72cm	67cm	33.5cm	5.9cm	14.6cm	9cm	4cm
76cm	71cm	35.5cm	6.3cm	15.5cm	9.5cm	4.2cm
82cm	77cm	38.5cm	6.9cm	17cm	10.2cm	4.4cm
88cm	83cm	41.5cm	7.5cm	18.5cm	11cm	4.5cm
94cm	89cm	44.5cm	8.6cm	19cm	11.9cm	4.6cm
100cm	95cm	47.5cm	9cm	21cm	12.8cm	4.7cm
104cm	99cm	49.5cm	9.5cm	22cm	13.2cm	4.8cm

1905 plunge front corset measurement table for the hips

Full hip measurement	Reduced hip measurement	Half reduced hip measurement	Panel 1	Panel 2	Panel 3	Panel 4
84cm	82cm	41cm	7.8cm	18.2cm	8.2cm	6.8cm
88cm	86cm	43cm	8.2cm	19.1cm	8.6cm	7.1cm
92cm	90cm	45cm	8.6cm	20cm	9cm	7.4cm
96cm	94cm	47cm	9cm	20.9cm	9.4cm	7.7cm
100cm	98cm	49cm	9.4cm	21.8cm	9.8cm	8cm
106cm	104cm	52cm	10cm	23cm	10.5cm	8.5cm
112cm	110cm	55cm	10.5cm	24.5cm	11cm	9cm
118cm	116cm	58cm	11.2cm	25.3cm	12cm	9.5cm
124cm	122cm	61cm	11.4cm	27cm	12.6cm	10cm
130cm	128cm	64cm	12cm	28.3cm	13.2cm	10.5cm

Create a table of measurements for your model

Create an individual table for your model to isolate the specific measurements required to draft your historical pattern. See example table below.

1905 plunge front corset individual measurement table example

Size	Full measurement	Reduced measurement	Half reduced measurement + bust gap	Panel 1	Panel 2	Panel 3	Panel 4
Bust	90cm	88cm	42cm	10.8cm	21.4cm	9.8cm	
Waist	68cm	63cm	31.5cm	5.5cm	13.8cm	8.3cm	3.9cm
Hip	100cm	98cm	49cm	9.4cm	21.8cm	9.8cm	8cm

Begin plotting the 1905 plunge front corset onto your traced basic block pattern

When drafting the **1905** corset pattern the **bust** measurements are plotted onto the **point to point** line and the **hip** measurements are plotted on the lower **mid-hip** line. When this does not apply it is highlighted within the pattern instructions.

Panel 1

3 to **13**	**waist** measurement
7 to **14**	**bust** measurement
14 to **13**	connect with a temporary straight line
14 to **15**	**1cm** on temporary line (**14** to **13**)
11 to **16**	**hip** measurement
16 to **17**	square up from point **16** with a temporary line to the **mid-hip** line to find point **17**
17 to **18**	one third measurement (**16** to **17**)
13 to **18**	connect with a straight line

Panel 4

4 to **19**	**waist** measurement
12 to **20**	**hip** measurement
20 to **21**	square up from point **20** to the **mid-hip** line to find point **21**
21 to **22**	half measurement (**20** to **21**)
4 to **23**	half measurement (**4** to **8**) minus **1cm** on **CF** line
23 to **24**	square across **4cm** with a temporary line

22 through **19** to temporary line (**23** to **24**) connect with a very shallow concave curve to find point **25**

23 to **25**	connect with a straight line

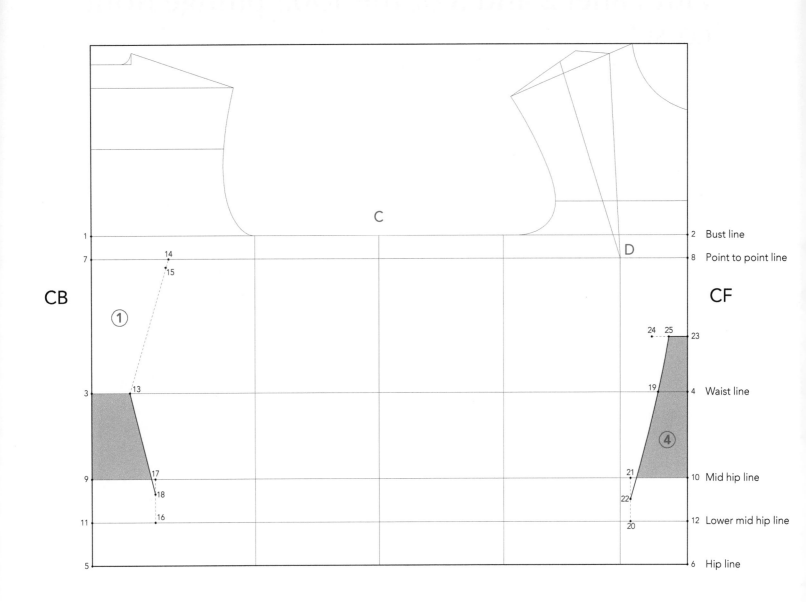

Plot Panel 2 and 3 of the 1905 plunge front corset

Panel 2

26 to **27**	**waist** measurement distribute equally either side of line **C**
27 to **28**	square up from point **27** to the **point to point** line to find point **28**
28 to **29**	square across **0.5cm** to the right of point **29**
29 to **30**	**bust** measurement
30 to **26**	connect with a temporary straight line
29 to **27**	connect with a temporary straight line
31 to **32**	**hip** measurement distribute three fifths of the **hip** measurement to the left of line **C** and two fifths of the **hip** measurement to the right of line **C**
32 to **33**	square up **0.5cm**
31 to **34**	square up to the **mid-hip** line to find point **33**

Measure line **13** to **18** on **Panel 1** transfer measurement to **Panel 2** from point **26** to find point **35** on line (**31** to **34**) – connect with a straight line

27 to **33**	connect with a temporary straight line

Panel 3

36	lies at the junction of the **waist**line and line **D**
36 to **37**	**waist** measurement to the left of line **D**
38	lies at the junction of the **bust** dart and **point** to **point** line
38 to **39**	**0.8cm**
39 to **40**	**bust** measurement
41	lies at the junction of the lower **mid-hip** line and line **D**
41 to **42**	**0.5cm** to the left of line **D**
42 to **43**	**hip** measurement
40 to **37**	connect with a temporary straight line
37 to **43**	connect with a temporary straight line
36 to **42**	connect with a very slight convex curve

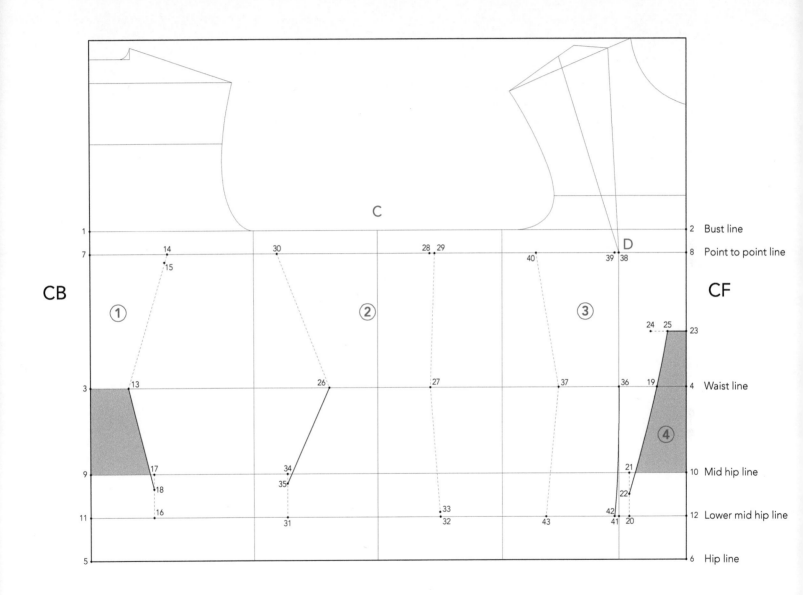

CB

CF

C

D

① ② ③ ④

2 Bust line
8 Point to point line
23
4 Waist line
10 Mid hip line
12 Lower mid hip line
6 Hip line

1
7
3
9
11
5

14
15
30
28 29
40
39 38
13
26
27
37
36 19
24 25
17
34
21
18
35
22
16
31
33
32
43
42
41 20

Shape the top of the 1905 plunge front corset pattern

Panel 1

7 to 44	**1.6cm** on **CB** line
13 to 45	one quarter measurement (**13** to **15**)
45 to 46	square across **0.3cm**

15 through 46 to 13 connect with a shallow concave curve

Panel 2

Measure temporary line 13 to 15 on **Panel 1** transfer measurement to **Panel 2** from point 26 to find point 47

26 to 48	one quarter measurement (**26** to **47**)
48 to 49	square across **0.3cm**

47 through 49 to 26 connect with a shallow concave curve

Ensure that line (**47** through **49** to **26**) is the same length as (**15** through **46** to **13**)

29 to 50	extend temporary line (**27** to **29**) to **0.5cm** beyond the **bust** line to find point **50**

27 to 51	one quarter measurement (**27** through **29** to **50**)
51 to 52	square across **0.3cm**

50 through 52 to 27 connect with a shallow concave curve (note: this may not go through point **29**)

Panel 3

Measure temporary line 27 through 29 to 50 on **Panel 2** transfer measurement to **Panel 3** from point 37 through 40 to find point 53

37 to 54	one quarter measurement (**37** through **40** to **53**)
54 to 55	square across **0.3cm**

53 through 55 to 37 connect with a shallow concave curve

Ensure that line (**53** through **55** to **37**) is the same length as (**50** through **52** to **27**)

53 to 56	two thirds measurement (**40** to **39**) on the **bust** line – transfer this measurement from point **53** to the bust line where this measurement hits the bust line is point **56**

Measure line **19** to **25** on **Panel 4** transfer measurement to **Panel 3** from point **36** to find point **57** on line **D**

57 to 58	half measurement (**38** to **57**)
58 to 59	square across **0.3cm**

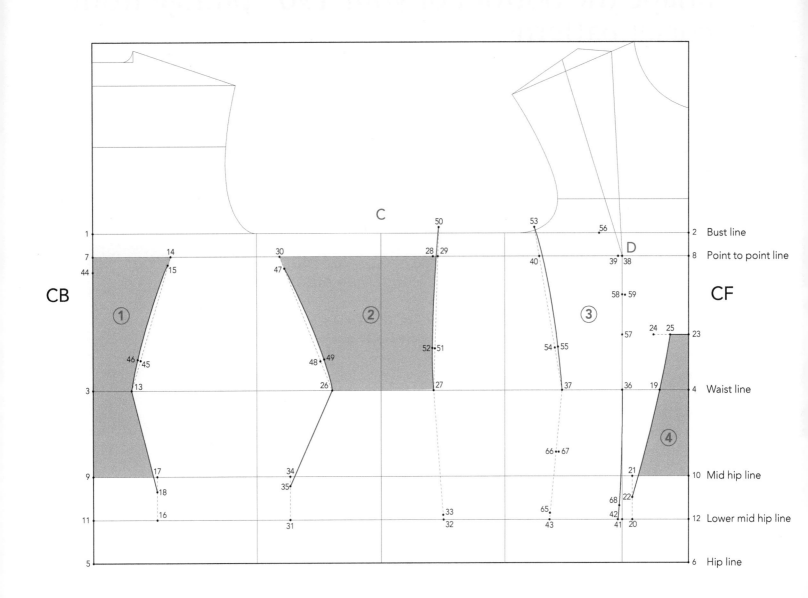

CB

CF

C

D

① ② ③ ④

1	2 Bust line
7	8 Point to point line
3	4 Waist line
9	10 Mid hip line
11	12 Lower mid hip line
5	6 Hip line

14
15
44
46 45
13
17
18
16

30
47
48 49
26
34
35
31

50
28 29
52 51
27
33
32

53
56
40
39 38
58 59
57
54 55
37
66 67
65
43

24 25 23
36 19
21
22
68
42
41 20

Shape the bottom of your 1905 plunge front corset pattern

Panel 1

9 to **60**   **0.6cm** on the **CB** line

Panel 2

61   lies at the junction of the **hip** line and line **C**

61 to **62**   **1cm** on **hip** line to the right of line **C**

27 to **63**   half measurement (**27** to **33**)

63 to **64**   square across **0.3cm**

27 through **64** to **33** connect with a very shallow concave curve

Panel 3

Measure temporary line **27** to **33** on **Panel 2** transfer measurement to **Panel 3** from point **37** to find point **65**

37 to **66**   half measurement (**37** to **65**)

66 to **67**   square across **0.3cm**

37 through **67** to **65** connect with a shallow concave curve

Ensure that line (**37** through **67** to **65**) is the same length as (**27** through **64** to **33**)

Measure line **19** to **22** on **Panel 4** transfer measurement to **Panel 3** from point **36** to find point **68**

Panel 4

6 to **69**   **1.2cm** on **CF** line

69 to **70**   square across with a temporary line half **waist** measurement (**4** to **19**)

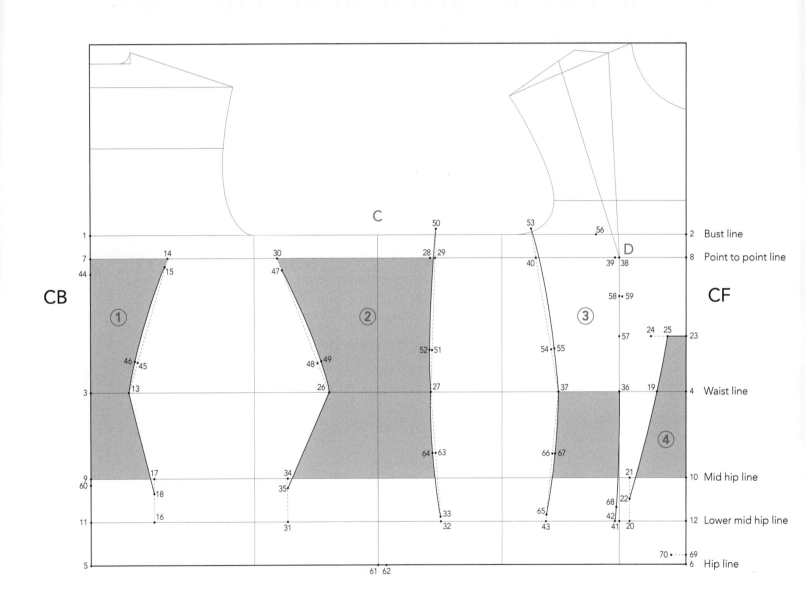

CB

CF

C

D

① ② ③ ④

1 — 2 Bust line

7 — 8 Point to point line

3 — 4 Waist line

9 — 10 Mid hip line

11 — 12 Lower mid hip line

5 — 6 Hip line

Connect the top and bottom of the 1905 plunge front corset pattern

1905 corset top line

Panel 1

44 to **15**   connect with a slight convex curve

Panel 2

47 to **50**   connect with a temporary straight line

47 to **71**   one quarter measurement (**47** to **50**)

50 to **72**   one quarter measurement (**47** to **50**)

72 to **73**   square up **0.6cm**

47 through **71**, **73** to **50** connect with a continuous convex curve using the diagram as a guide

Panel 3

53 through **56**, **39** and **59** to **57** connect with a continuous line using the diagram as a guide

57 to **36**   connect with a straight line

1905 corset bottom line

Panel 1

60 to **18**   connect with a slight convex curve

Panel 2

35 to **62**   connect with a slight convex curve

33 to **62**   connect with a straight line

Panel 3

65 to **68**   connect with a very shallow concave curve

Panel 4

22 to **70**   connect with a temporary straight line

74   lies at the junction of the lower **mid-hip** line and temporary line (**22** to **70**)

74 to **75**   square up **0.5cm**

22 through **75** to **70** connect with a shallow concave curve

70 to **69**   connect with a straight line

Round off the corner at point **70**

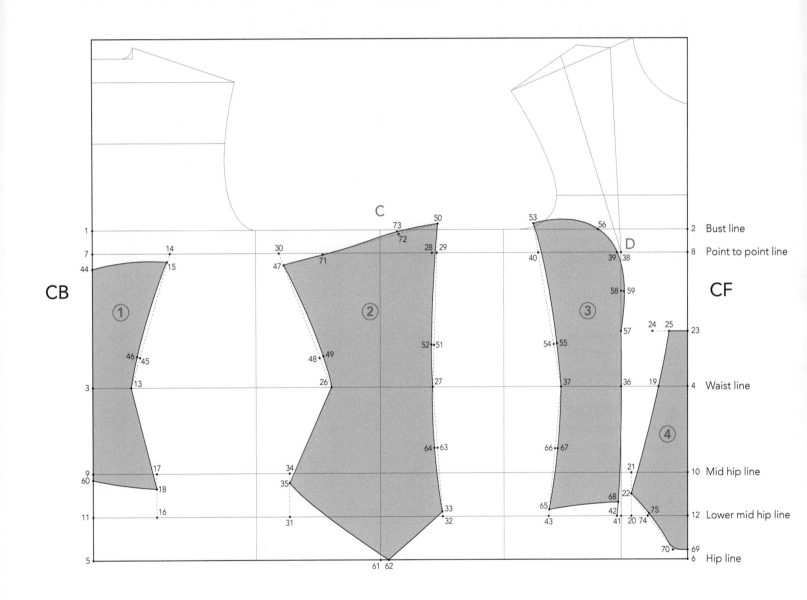

CB

CF

C

D

Bust line
Point to point line
Waist line
Mid hip line
Lower mid hip line
Hip line

Draw the bone channels on your completed 1905 plunge front corset pattern

Use the diagram as a guide when drawing in your bone channels, these are **0.8cm** wide with bones that are **0.6cm** wide. If you wish you can use a **1cm** wide bone channel with a **0.7cm** wide bone. At the centre back there is a central eyelet channel that is **1.3cm** wide on both sides for lacing up the corset. The original corset has two wide bones on **Panel 2**; these have been replaced with two narrower bones as wider bones are not always available. The front panel has a busk channel that is **1.3cm** wide and rows of top stitching.

When tracing your pattern mark the number on each panel and the **waist** position to help you identify them accurately and align each piece when sewing your corset together. Each half of the corset connects in numerical order as they are seen on the pattern.

Panel 3 points **57** to **68** will be sewn to **Panel 4** points **25** to **22**.

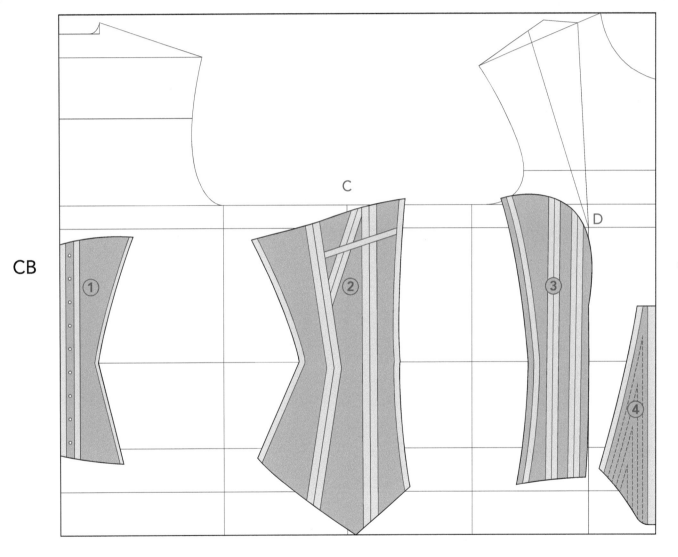

15 1915 deep skirted corset

1915 deep skirted corset

This deep skirted corset dated 1915 is part of the Symington Corsetry collection held in Leicestershire. The corset is originally from the USA and is stamped "R&G D223 rustless boning"; it was possibly purchased as a sample. The corset has fourteen panels and is made from cotton batiste. It has a 7.5cm (3 inches) deep slotted lace trim that goes around the top edge of the corset, with a large decorative bow and pull cords that could be adjusted by the wearer for a better fit under the bust. The corset also has six adjustable suspenders with metal clasps and covered buttons.

The 1915 corset is extremely long 50cm (19.5 inches) at the centre back and 40cm (16 inches) at the centre front. It is only 10cm (4 inches) above the waist with a long skirt that is 40cm (16 inches) fitting low over the thighs. The bottom of the corset at the centre front has a shorter panel that overlaps allowing more movement whilst worn. The back steels are 44.5cm (17.5 inches) and the centre front has a steel busk with two hooks and eyes sewn below. The waist measurement is 51cm (20 inches), hips 92cm (36.5 inches).

The fashion for a version of the empire line between 1910 and 1915 resulted in extremely narrow skirts with a higher waistline. Although fashions claimed to liberate women's waists from the very tight lacing at the waist, the long skirt that stretched over the hips and down the thighs restricted movement of the legs and this made walking with anything more than small steps very difficult.

The corset followed the fashionable line with a deep skirt fitting almost to the knees. The straighter line of the corset meant that the hip and bust gussets from the previous decade were no longer required. The slender figure meant that the corset was often so long and tight that it was not only extremely uncomfortable, it was also almost impossible for the wearer to sit down.

Opposite: The panels of 1915 deep skirted corset are designed to lengthen the body to create a long slim silhouette.

Original 1915 deep skirted corset pattern

The lines on the 1915 historical corset pattern diagram opposite are a guide for drafting the new pattern onto the female basic block. The approximate position of the **point to point** line, **waist**line and **hip** line are shown on the diagram, it is also labelled with the **CB** and **CF** and lines **A, B, C, D, E** which are additional guidelines for the position of **Panel 2**, **Panel 3**, **Panel 4**, **Panel 5** and **Panel 6**.

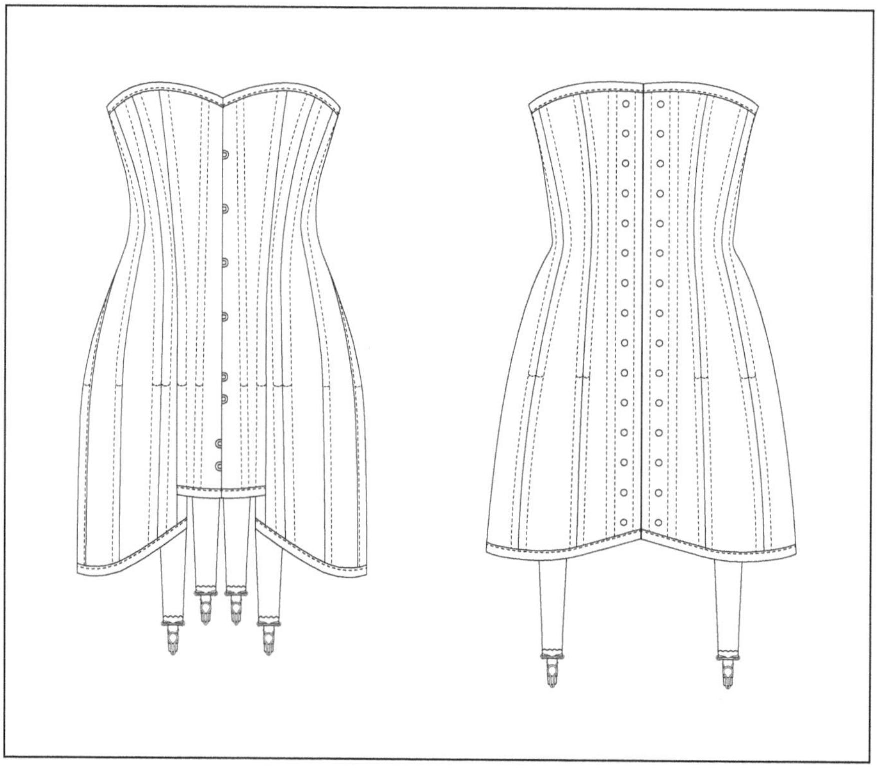

The front and back views of the original 1915 deep skirted corset show the seam lines, bone channels, front busk and suspenders.

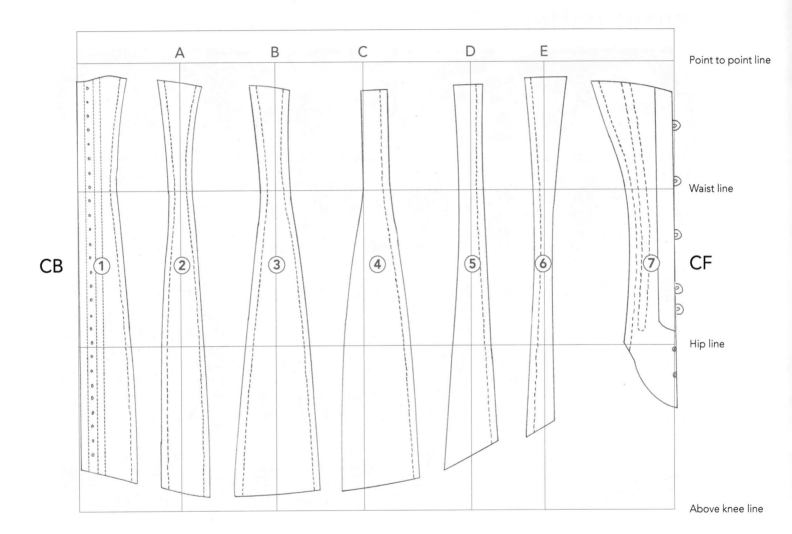

CB   A   B   C   D   E   CF

Point to point line

Waist line

Hip line

Above knee line

Guidelines for the 1915 deep skirted corset pattern

Trace and separate the female basic block pattern following the instructions in Chapter 5, 'Preparing the female basic block for your historic pattern'. Leave a gap of **30cm** between the basic block back side seam and basic block front side seam and number each line.

Draw in the following additional guidelines

7 to **8**   **point to point** line

The **point to point** line lies at the base of the **bust** dart square across from the **CB** line to the **CF** line

9 to **10**   **above knee** line

Extend your female basic block pattern by the measurement between the **waist**line (**3** to **4**) and **hip** line (**5** to **6**) to find the **above knee** line (**9** to **10**). Square across from the **CB** line to the **CF** line

11 to **12** **lower mid-hip** line

The **lower mid-hip** line lies half measurement (**5** to **9**) on the **CB** line square across from the **CB** line to the **CF** line

Extend the original side back seam, side front seam and line **C** down to the **above knee** line

Line **D**   mark your traced female basic block original extended back side seam line **D**

Front lace detail of the 1915 deep skirted corset

From the collections of Leicester County Counci l: Symington Collection. England.

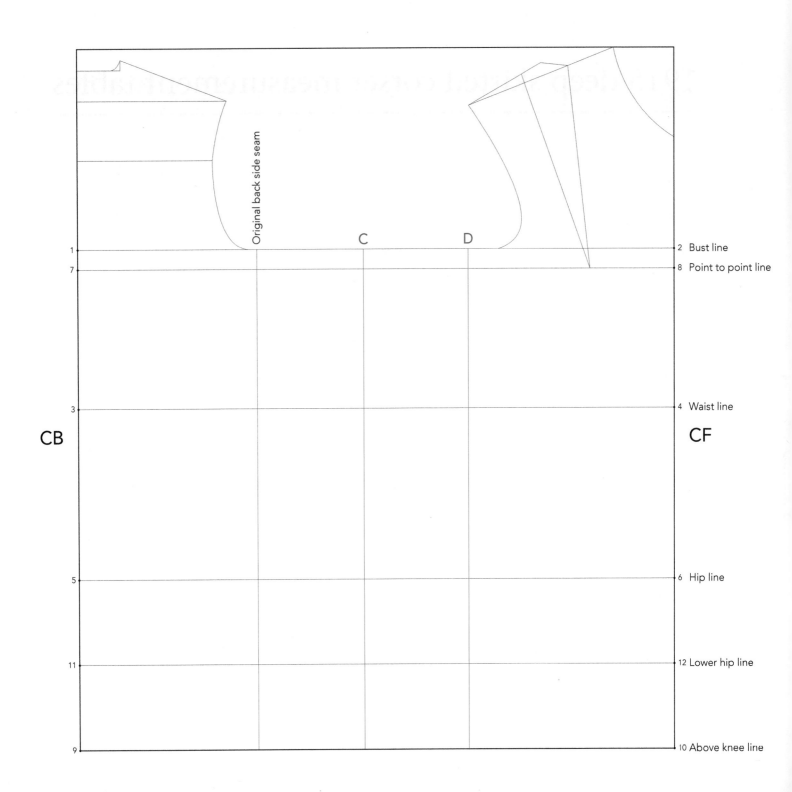

CB

CF

Original back side seam

C   D

1   2 Bust line

7   8 Point to point line

3   4 Waist line

5   6 Hip line

11   12 Lower hip line

9   10 Above knee line

1915 deep skirted corset measurement tables

The tables below contain measurements for each pattern piece. Find the **bust**, **waist** and **hip** measurements that are the closest to that of your model. The calculation for the size of each panel is recorded horizontally to these measurements.

1915 deep skirted corset measurement table for the bust

Bust measurement	Reduced bust measurement	Half reduced bust measurement	Panel 1	Panel 2	Panel 3	Panel 4	Panel 5	Panel 6	Panel 7
80cm	77cm	38.5cm	6cm	5.3cm	5cm	3.8cm	3.6cm	5.2cm	9.6cm
82cm	79cm	39.5cm	6.2cm	5.4cm	5.1cm	3.9cm	3.6cm	5.3cm	10cm
86cm	83cm	41.5cm	6.5cm	5.7cm	5.4cm	4.1cm	3.8cm	5.6cm	10.4cm
90cm	87cm	43.5cm	6.8cm	6cm	5.6cm	4.3cm	4.2cm	5.8cm	10.8cm
94cm	91cm	45.5cm	7.1cm	6.3cm	5.8cm	4.5cm	4.4cm	6.1cm	11.3cm
100cm	97cm	48.5cm	7.6cm	6.7cm	6.3cm	4.7cm	4.6cm	6.6cm	12cm
106cm	103cm	51.5cm	8cm	7.2cm	6.6cm	5cm	4.9cm	7cm	12.8cm
112cm	109cm	54.5cm	8.6cm	7.5cm	7cm	5.3cm	5.1cm	7.4cm	13.6cm
118cm	115cm	57.5cm	9cm	8cm	7.4cm	5.6cm	5.5cm	7.8cm	14.2cm
124cm	121cm	60.5cm	9.4cm	8.3cm	7.9cm	6.1cm	5.8cm	8cm	15cm

1915 deep skirted corset measurement table for the waist

Full waist measurement	Reduced waist measurement	Half reduced waist measurement	Panel 1	Panel 2	Panel 3	Panel 4	Panel 5	Panel 6	Panel 7
62cm	57cm	28.5cm	5.2cm	3.4cm	4.1cm	3.6cm	3.4cm	2.5cm	6.3cm
64cm	59cm	29.5cm	5.4cm	3.6cm	4.2cm	3.7cm	3.5cm	2.6cm	6.5cm
68cm	63cm	31.5cm	5.7cm	3.8cm	4.5cm	3.9cm	3.7cm	2.7cm	7.2cm
72cm	67cm	33.5cm	6.1cm	4cm	4.8cm	4.1cm	3.9cm	2.9cm	7.7cm
76cm	71cm	35.5cm	6.5cm	4.3cm	5.2cm	4.3cm	4.3cm	3.1cm	7.8cm
82cm	77cm	38.5cm	7.1cm	4.8cm	5.8cm	4.6cm	4.4cm	3.4cm	8.4cm
88cm	83cm	41.5cm	7.7cm	5.3cm	6.2cm	4.9cm	4.6cm	3.6cm	9.2cm
94cm	89cm	44.5cm	8.1cm	6cm	6.5cm	5.2cm	4.8cm	3.9cm	10cm
100cm	95cm	47.5cm	8.7cm	6.3cm	6.8cm	5.7cm	5.4cm	4.1cm	10.5cm
104cm	99cm	49.5cm	9cm	6.4cm	7.2cm	6.1cm	5.7cm	4.2cm	10.9cm

1915 deep skirted corset measurement table for the hips

Full hip measurement	Half hip measurement	Panel 1	Panel 2	Panel 3	Panel 4	Panel 5	Panel 6	Panel 7
84cm	42cm	6.2cm	5.7cm	8cm	8cm	4.9cm	2.6cm	6.6cm
88cm	44cm	6.4cm	6cm	8.4cm	8.4cm	5.2cm	2.7cm	6.9cm
92cm	46cm	6.7cm	6.3cm	8.7cm	8.7cm	5.4cm	2.8cm	7.4cm
96cm	48cm	7.1cm	6.5cm	9.2cm	9.2cm	5.5cm	3cm	7.6cm
100cm	50cm	7.4cm	6.8cm	9.5cm	9.5cm	5.8cm	3.1cm	7.9cm
106cm	53cm	7.8cm	7.2cm	10cm	10cm	6cm	3.4cm	8.6cm
112cm	56cm	8.2cm	7.6cm	10.6cm	10.6cm	6.2cm	3.6cm	9.2cm
118cm	59cm	8.6cm	7.9cm	11cm	11cm	6.5cm	3.9cm	10.1cm
124cm	62cm	9.6cm	8.7cm	11.6cm	11.6cm	6.6cm	4.1cm	10.6cm
130cm	65cm	9.5cm	8.6cm	12.4cm	12.4cm	6.7cm	4.2cm	11cm

Create a table of measurements for your model

Create an individual table for your model to isolate the specific measurements required to draft your historical pattern. See example table below.

1915 deep skirted corset individual measurement table example

Size	Full measurement	Reduced measurement	Half reduced measurement	Panel 1	Panel 2	Panel 3	Panel 4	Panel 5	Panel 6	Panel 7
Bust	86cm	83cm	41.5cm	6.5cm	5.7cm	5.4cm	4.1cm	3.8cm	5.6cm	10.4cm
Waist	76cm	71cm	35.5cm	6.5cm	4.3cm	5.2cm	4.3cm	4.3cm	3.1cm	7.8cm
Hip	112cm	112cm	56cm	8.2cm	7.6cm	10.6cm	10.6cm	6.2cm	3.6cm	9.2cm

Begin plotting the 1915 deep skirted corset onto your traced basic block pattern

When drafting the **1915** corset pattern the **bust** measurements are plotted onto the **point to point** line and the **hip** measurements are plotted onto the **hip** line. When this does not apply it is highlighted within the pattern instructions.

Panel 1

3 to **13**	**waist** measurement
7 to **14**	**bust** measurement
5 to **15**	**hip** measurement
14 to **13**	connect with a straight line
13 to **15**	connect with a temporary straight line

Panel 7

4 to **16**	**waist** measurement
8 to **17**	**bust** measurement
6 to **18**	**hip** measurement
17 to **16**	connect with a temporary straight line
16 to **18**	connect with a very shallow concave curve

Panel 4

19	lies at the junction of the **waist**line (**3** to **4**) and line **C**
19 to **20**	**waist** measurement to the right of line **C**
21	lies at the junction of the **point to point** line (**7** to **8**) and line **C**
21 to **22**	**bust** measurement to the right of line **C**
23 to **24**	**hip** measurement distribute one third **hip** measurement to the left of line **C** and two thirds **hip** measurement to the right of line **C**
21 to **19**	connect with a straight line
19 to **23**	connect with a slight convex curve
22 to **20**	connect with a straight line
20 to **24**	connect with a slight convex curve

Draw in the following additional guideline

Line **A**	on the **waist**line mark half measurement between point **13** and the original basic block back side seam – square up to **bust** line and down to **above knee** line

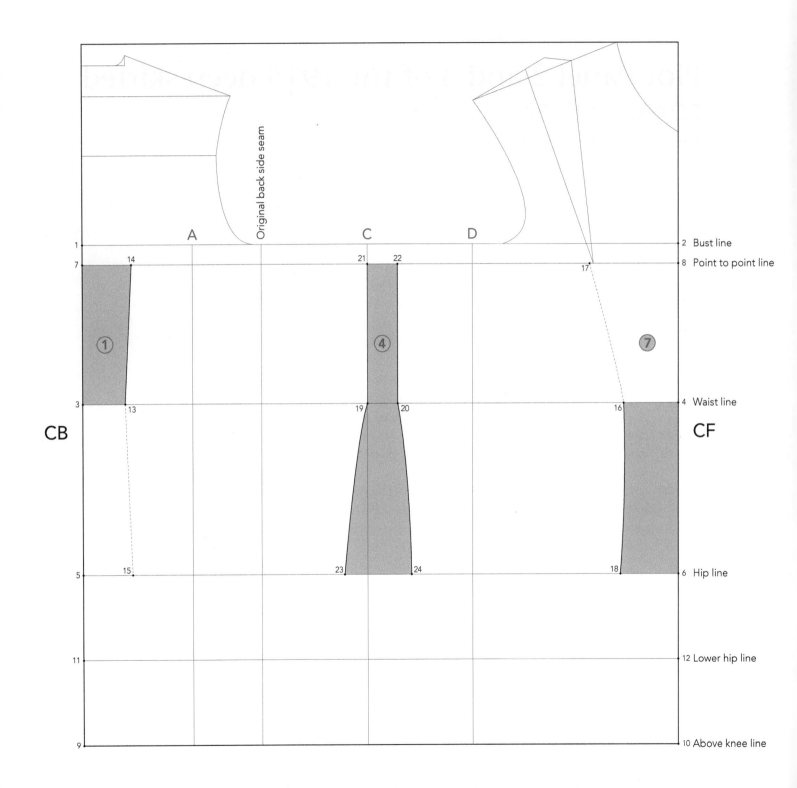

Plot Panel 2 and 3 of the 1915 deep skirted corset pattern

Panel 2

25 to **26**	**waist** measurement distribute equally either side of line **A**
27 to **28**	**bust** measurement distribute two fifths **bust** measurement to the left of line **A** and three fifths **bust** measurement to the right of line **A**
29 to **30**	**hip** measurement distribute equally either side of line **A**
27 to **25**	connect with a straight line
25 to **29**	connect with a temporary straight line
28 to **26**	connect with a very shallow concave curve
26 to **30**	connect with a slight convex curve

Draw in the following additional guideline

Line **B**	on the **hip** line mark half measurement (**30** to **23**) square up to **bust** line and down to the **above knee** line

Panel 3

31 to **32**	**waist** measurement distribute equally either side of line **B**
33 to **34**	**bust** measurement distribute three fifths **bust** measurement to the left of line **B** and two fifths **bust** measurement to the right of line **B**
35 to **36**	hip measurement distribute three fifths **hip** measurement to the left of line **B** and two fifths **hip** measurement to the right of line **B**
33 to **31**	connect with a very shallow concave curve
31 to **35**	connect with a slight convex curve
34 to **32**	connect with a straight line
32 to **36**	connect with a slight convex curve

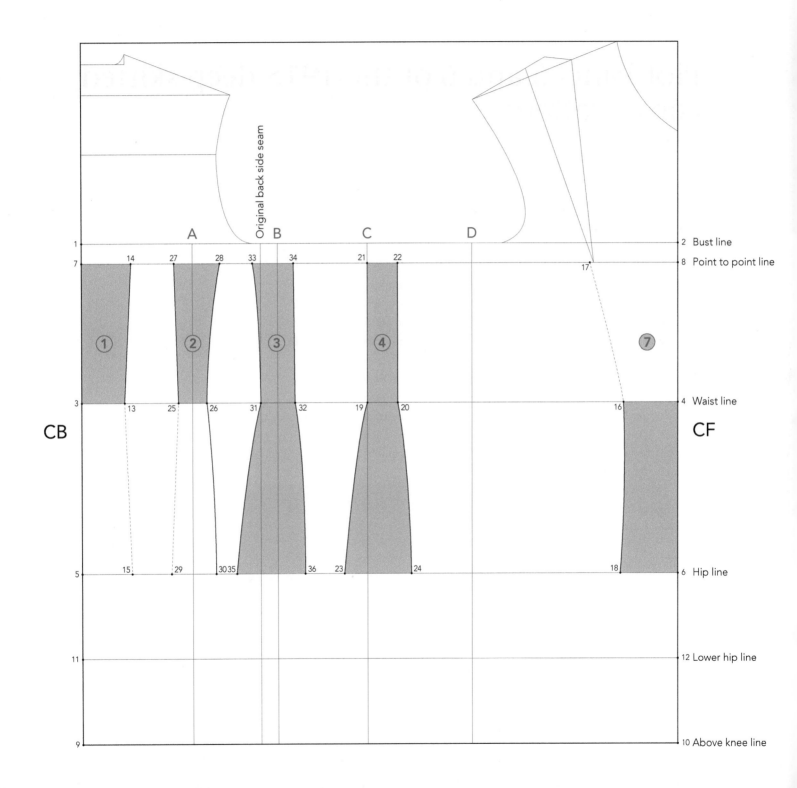

Plot Panel 5 and 6 of the 1915 deep skirted corset pattern

Panel 5

37 to **38**	**waist** measurement distribute equally either side of line **D**
39 to **40**	**bust** measurement distribute equally either side of line **D**
41 to **42**	**hip** measurement distribute half **hip** measurement plus **0.5cm** to the left of line **D** and half **hip** measurement minus **0.5cm** to the right of line **D**
39 to **37**	connect with a straight line
37 to **41**	connect with a slight convex curve
40 to **38**	connect with a straight line
38 to **42**	connect with a straight line

Draw in the following additional guideline

Line **E**	on the **waist**line mark half measurement (**38** to **16**) square up to **bust** line and down to the **above knee** line

Panel 6

43 to **44**	**waist** measurement distribute equally either side of line **E**
45 to **46**	**bust** measurement distribute equally either side of line **E**
47 to **48**	**hip** measurement distribute equally either side of line **E**
45 to **43**	connect with a straight line
43 to **47**	connect with a straight line
46 to **44**	connect with a temporary straight line
44 to **48**	onnect with a straight line

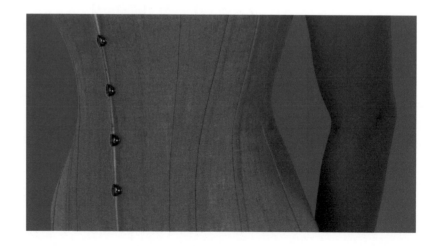

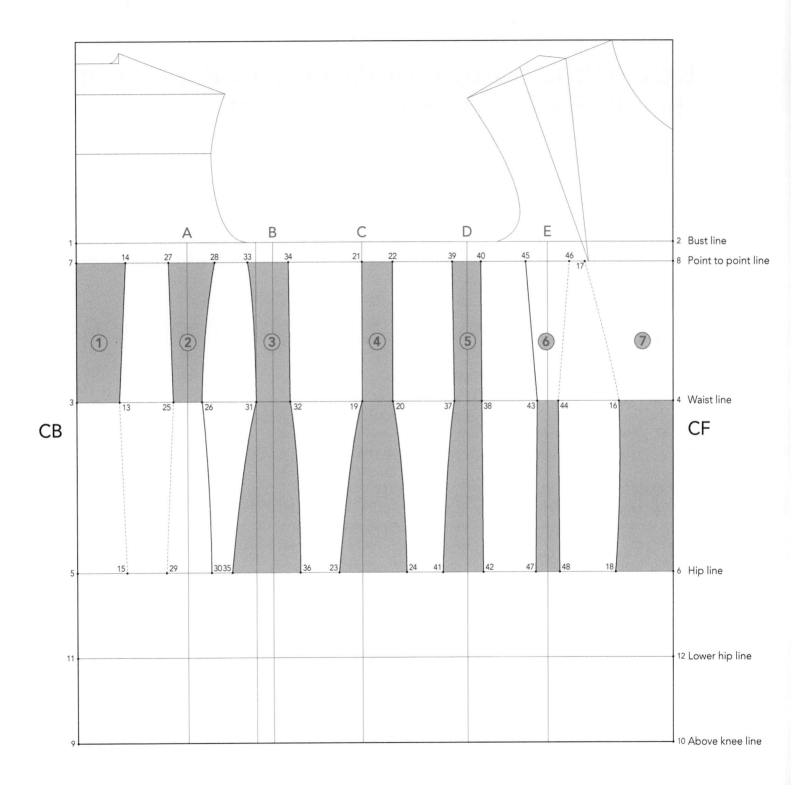

Extend the bottom of Panel 1 to Panel 3 of the 1915 deep skirted corset pattern

Panel 1

11 to **49**   half measurement (**11** to **9**) on the **CB** line

15 to **50**   extend line (**13** to **15**) to the **above knee** line to find point **50**

15 to **51**   square across **0.5cm**

13 through **51** to **50** connect with a slight convex curve

50 to **52**   one third measurement (**9** to **11**) on the **CF** to find point **52**

Panel 2

29 to **53**   extend line (**25** to **29**) to the **above knee** line to find point **53**

29 to **54**   square across **0.5cm**

25 through **54** to **53** connect with a slight convex curve

Measure temporary line **13** to **52** on **Panel 1** transfer measurement to **Panel 2** from point **25** through **29** to find point **55**

Ensure that line (**25** through **54** to **55**) is the same length as (**13** through **51** to **52**)

30 to **56**   extend line (**26** to **30**) to the **above knee** line and across **0.5cm** towards the **CF** to find point **56**

56 to **57**   **1.5cm**

Panel 3

35 to **58**   extend line (**31** to **35**) to the **above knee** line and across **0.5cm** towards the **CB** to find point **58**

Measure line **26** through **30** to **57** on **Panel 2** transfer measurement to **Panel 3** from point **31** through **35** to find point **59**

36 to **60**   extend line (**32** to **36**) to the **above knee** line and across **0.5cm** towards the **CF** to find point **60**

60 to **61**   **2.5cm**

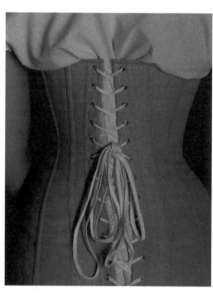

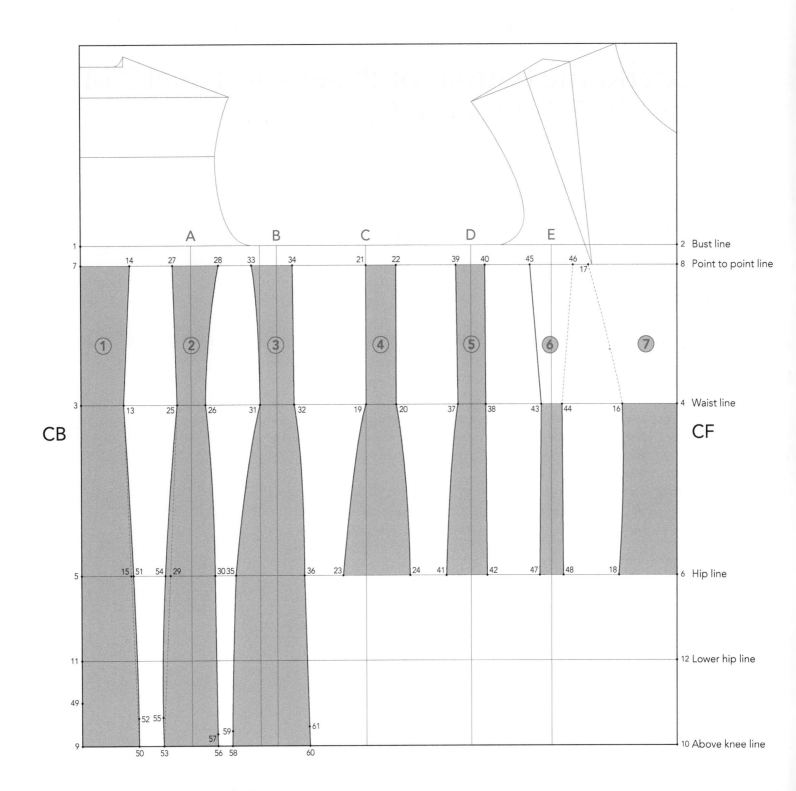

Extend the bottom of Panel 4 to Panel 7 of the 1915 deep skirted corset pattern

Panel 4

23 to **62**   extend line (**19** to **23**) to the **above knee** line and across **0.5cm** towards the **CB** to find point **62**

Measure line **32** through **36** to **61** on **Panel 3** transfer measurement to **Panel 4** from point **19** through **23** to find point **63**

24 to **64**   extend line (**20** to **24**) to the **above knee** line and across **0.5cm** towards the **CF** to find point **64**

64 to **65**   one third measurement **12** to **10**) on the **CF** line to find point **65**

Panel 5

41 to **66**   extend line (**37** to **41**) to **above knee** line to find point **66**

Measure line **20** through **24** to **65** on **Panel 4** transfer measurement to **Panel 5** from point **37** through **41** to find point **67**

42 to **68**   extend line (**38** to **42**) to **above knee** line to find point **68**

68 to **69**   two thirds measurement (**10** to **12**) on the **CF** line to find point **69**

Panel 6

47 to **70**   extend line (**43** to **47**) to **above knee** line to find point **70**

Measure line **38** through **42** to **69** on **Panel 5** transfer measurement to **Panel 6** from point **43** through **47** to find point **71**

48 to **72**   extend line (**44** to **48**) to **above knee** line to find point **72**

73   lies at the junction of line (**11** to **12**) **lower hip** line and line (**48** to **72**)

Panel 7

12 to **74**   one fifth (**6** to **12**) on the **CF** line

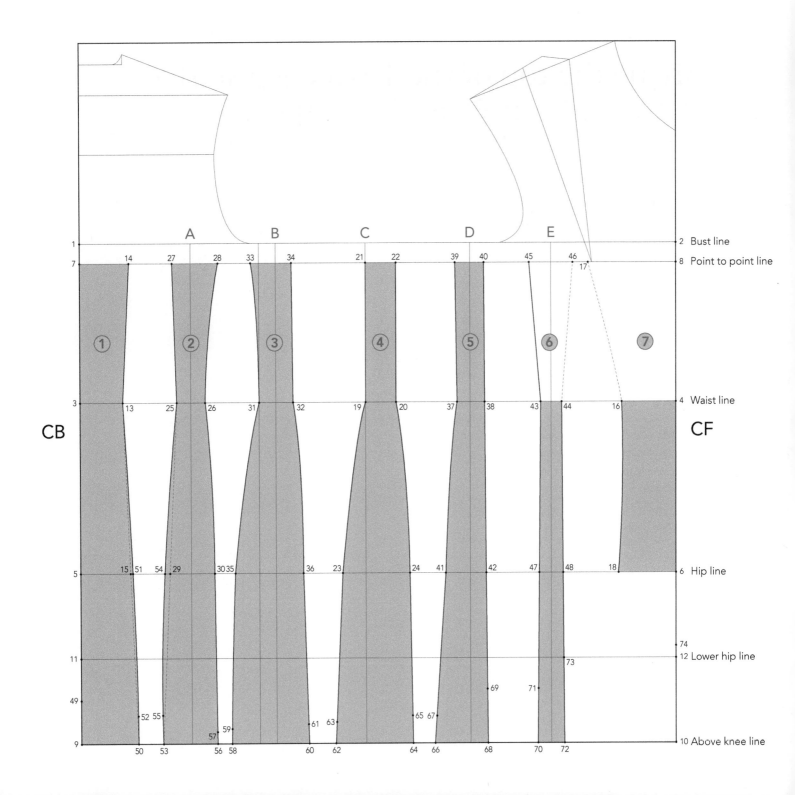

Shape the top of the 1915 deep skirted corset pattern Panel 1 to Panel 4

Panel 1

7 to **75**   **1.5cm** on **CB** line

14 to **76**   **1cm**

Panel 2

Measure line **13** to **76** on **Panel 1** transfer measurement to **Panel 2** from point **25** to find point **77**

28 to **78**   **1.5cm**

Panel 3

Measure line **26** to **78** on **Panel 2** transfer measurement to **Panel 3** from point **31** to find point **79**

34 to **80**   **2cm**

Panel 4

Measure line **32** to **80** on **Panel 3** transfer measurement to **Panel 4** from point **19** to find point **81**

22 to **82**   **2cm**

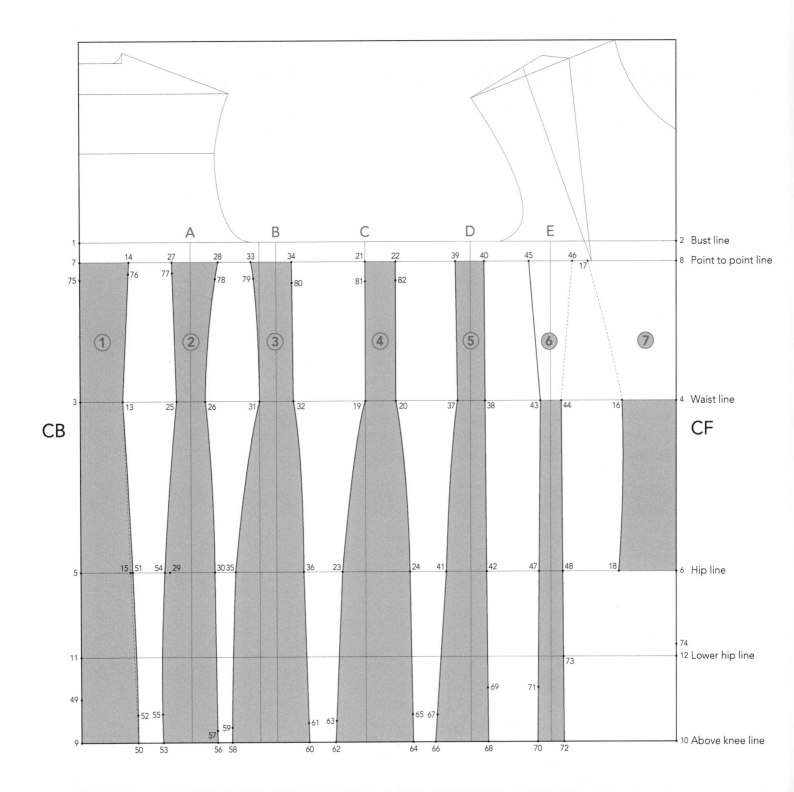

Shape the top of Panel 5 to Panel 7

Panel 5

Measure line **20** to **82** on **Panel 4** transfer measurement to **Panel 5** from point **37** to find point **83**

40 to **84**   **1.8cm**

Panel 6

Measure line **38** to **84** on **Panel 5** transfer measurement to **Panel 6** from point **43** to find point **85**

44 to **86**   half measurement line
                  (**44** to **46**)
86 to **87**   square across **0.5cm**

46 through **87** to **44** connect with a shallow concave curve

46 to **88**   **1.2cm**

Panel 7

16 to **89**   half measurement line (**16** to **17**)
89 to **90**   square across **0.5cm**

17 through **90** to **16** connect with a shallow concave curve

Measure line **44** through **87** to **88** on **Panel 6** transfer measurement to **Panel 7** from point **16** through **90** to find point **91**

8 to **92**   one quarter measurement (**8** to **4**) on **CF** line

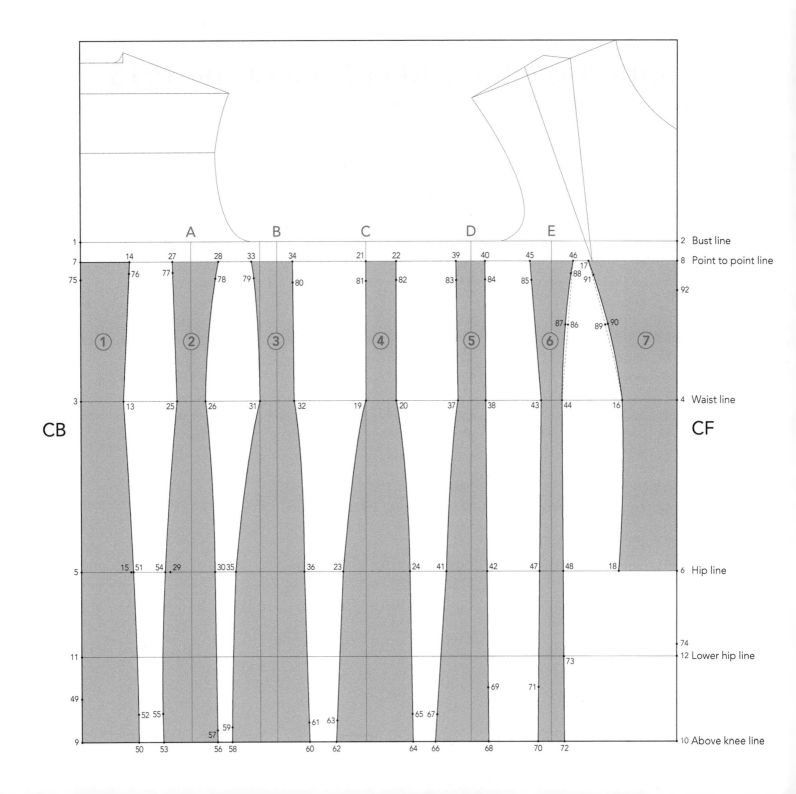

Connect the top and bottom of the 1915 deep skirted corset pattern

1915 corset top line

Panel 1
75 to **76** connect with a slight convex curve

Panel 2
77 to **78** connect with a slight convex curve

Panel 3
79 to **80** connect with a very slight convex curve

Panel 4
81 to **82** connect with a straight line

Panel 5
83 to **84** connect with a straight line

Panel 6
85 to **88** connect with a slight convex curve

Panel 7
91 to **92** connect with a slight convex curve

1915 corset bottom line

Panel 1
49 to **52** connect with a shallow concave curve

Panel 2
55 to **57** connect with a slight convex curve

Panel 3
59 to **61** connect with a slight convex curve

Panel 4
63 to **65** connect with a slight convex curve

Panel 5
67 to **69** connect with a slight convex curve

Panel 6
48 to **93** 5cm
71 to **73** connect with a very slight convex curve

Panel 7
18 to **94** **5cm**
18 to **74** connect with a temporary straight line
74 to **95** one third measurement (**18** to **74**)
95 to **96** square down **1.3cm**

18 through **96** to **74** connect with a continuous curve

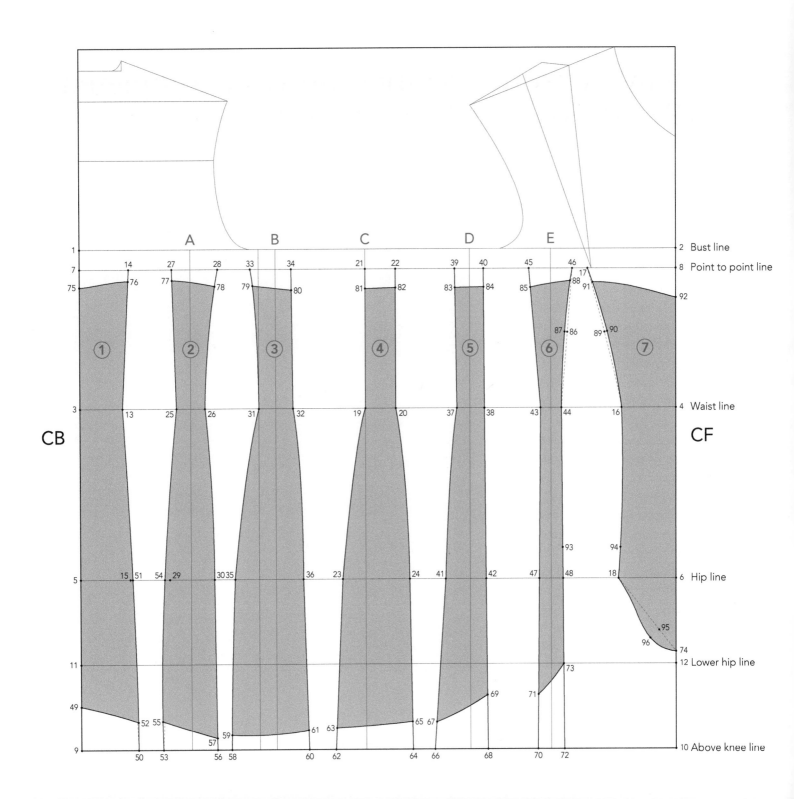

Draw the bone channels on your completed 1915 deep skirted corset pattern

Use the diagram as a guide to draw in your corset bone channels, these only go as far as the **hip** line to enable the wearer greater movement. The bone channels for the 1915 Deep Skirted Corset are **1cm** wide with a **0.7cm** wide bone. The centre back has two bone channels with a central eyelet channel that is **1.3cm** wide on both sides for lacing up the corset. The busk channel at the centre front is **1.3cm** wide.

When tracing your pattern mark the number on each panel and the **waist** position to help you identify them accurately and align each piece when sewing your corset together. Each half of the corset connects in numerical order as they are seen on the pattern. The front **panel 7** and adjacent **panel 6** join to just above the hip line, this allows greater freedom of movement for the wearer. The position where these panels join is marked on the pattern and below; all other panels are sewn down to the hemline.

Panel 6 points **88** to **93** will be sewn to
Panel 7 points **91** to **94**

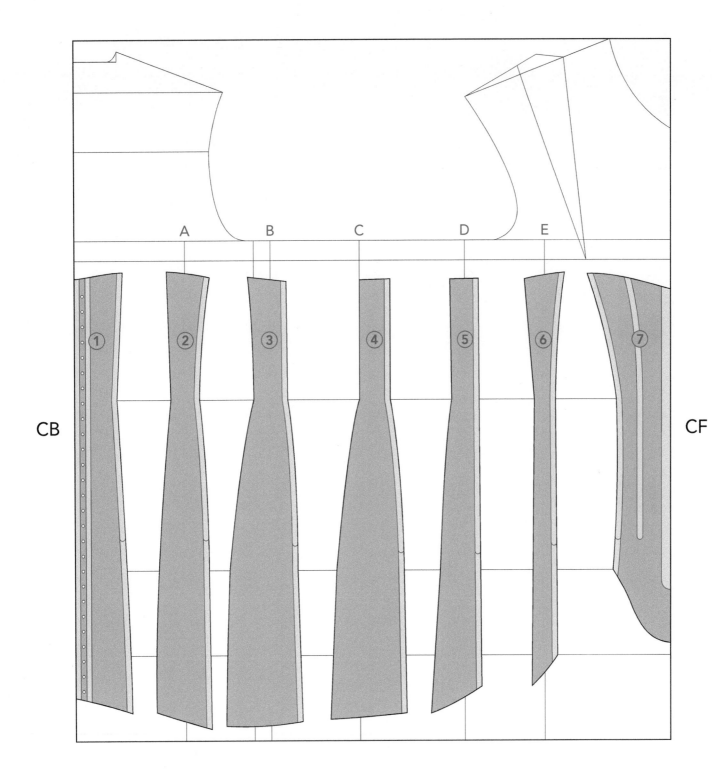

Glossary

Basic block a pattern that uses the individual measurements of the body to create a form-fitting pattern. The basic block can be adapted to create other pattern shapes

Bias tape a fabric strip cut at a 45 degree angle so it can go around a curve, often used to bind the edges of corsets

Bloomers an undergarment worn over the lower part of the body to cover each leg to the knee

Bodice a close fitting garment for the upper part of the body. It is also recognised as the top half of a dress but can be separate to the skirt

Bum roll a crescent shaped pad worn at the waist under the skirt to give fullness

Busk a piece of wood, whalebone or steel inserted at the centre front of the stays or corset to stiffen the garment

Camisole a short undergarment made from either cotton or silk that is fitted to the waist

Casing strips of fabric that are stitched to the garment to hold stay and corset bones in place

Chemise classic smock worn as an undergarment

Combinations Victorian underwear that combined bloomers with a camisole top

Corset boning strips of either cane, whalebone or steel used to shape and stiffen stays and corsets and control the silhouette

Corset bone channel tape a tubular tape that can be sewn to your corset and holds the corset bone in place

Corset a close fitting bodice stiffened originally with whalebone or reeds and later with steels – the term corset was used from the 19th century onwards, before which they were called stays

Corset lace woven cord or ribbon that threads through the eyelets to draw in the two sides of the corset

Crinoline a 19th-century petticoat stiffened with either horsehair, whalebone, cane or steel

Eyelets holes made either side of the centre back or centre front to lace up the stays or corset

Fabric grain the direction of the fabric's weave

False backs false backs are separate eyeleted and boned panels that are sewn on to a bodice or corset in order to fasten them for a fitting. These are removed after the fitting and can be re-used for other fittings.

Gusset a piece of fabric inserted to make a garment fuller, used in a corset at the bust and hips

Lasting a durable cloth of twisted yarn

Pair of bodies 16th-century corset

Panniers petticoat stiffened with hoops that creates a wide shallow silhouette

Pocket hoops a pair of 3D pockets with hoops worn on either hip to enhance the width of the skirt

Shaping bones extra whalebone placed in strips across the corset to create a conical shape

Spoon busk a shaped busk developed in 1880 to put less pressure on the abdomen

Stays a term used for 17th- and 18th-century corsets

Steam moulding wet starch applied to corset and then heated on a specially shaped female block to give corsets their final shape

Stomacher a boned triangular piece of fabric worn either behind or over front laced stays

Suspenders long pieces of elastic attached to corsets or suspender belts that is used to hold up stockings

Tabs shaped pieces of fabric created by slitting the stays around the hemline to add width

Waist tape a strong piece of ribbon, often grosgrain that is placed around the point of pressure on the corset, the waist

Pattern drafting glossary

CB the back half of the pattern that finishes at the spine in the centre of the body

CF the front half of the pattern that finishes at the breast bone in the centre of the body

Concave an inward curved line

Convex an outward curved line

Dart a triangular shape that is used to remove fabric to create a three-dimensional shape

Ease the difference between the actual body measurements and the size of the pattern

Nape the back of the neck

Square across measure or draw a line horizontally at a 90 degree angle to the original point

Square down measure or draw a line down at a 90 degree angle from the original point

Straight of grain relates to the weave of the fabric. This lies parallel to the warp threads and the selvedge

Suppression used to describe the shaping of the waist on the female basic block

Corset busks and boning

The materials used to construct a corset provide the structure and strength required to shape and control the body. Willow, ivory and whalebone used to stiffen both stays and corsets during the 17th, 18th and 19th centuries are no longer used and have been replaced with steel and plastic boning. The range of corset materials available to the corset maker has greatly increased over the past few years. Here are some examples of busks and bones, both steel and plastic, of varying widths and designs. The choice of boning used will depend on the date of the stays or corset, the authenticity, control and comfort required.

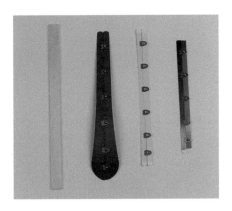

Busks: from right to left, straight wooden busk, spoon busk, straight split metal busk and lightweight metal busk with tipped ends

Various widths of straight metal bone; the narrowest is 5.5mm, the widest is 1.2cm. These are available in cut lengths or on a continuous roll that can be cut to size.

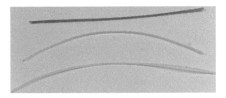

Plastic boning, also known as faux whalebone, comes in various widths, both flat and elliptical. This is easily cut to size and provides lightweight boning.

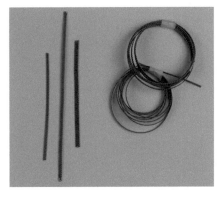

Spiral bones of various widths; the narrowest is 5mm, the widest is 1cm. These also come in cut lengths with end caps or on a continuous roll that can be cut to size and end caps added.

Corset lace with metal ends; these come in various colours and lengths.

Metal eyelets and specialist hooks and bars. The two-part eyelet and washer are used to reinforce holes punched through the corset for lacing up the garment. The two-part hook and eye fastenings are used to fasten the top and bottom of a corset above and below the length of the busk.

Costume collections

Listed below are museums that have supported my research and study of the historical garments within their significant costume collections.

The Bavarian National Museum
Prinzregentenstraße 3,
80538 München,
Germany
http://www.bayerisches-nationalmuseum.de/

Fashion Museum Bath
Bath Assembly Rooms,
Bennett Street,
Bath, BA1 2QH
http://www.museumofcostume.co.uk/

Hampshire Arts and Museum Services
Department of Culture, Community and Business Services
Chilcombe House
Chilcomb Lane
Winchester, SO23 8RD
https://www.hampshireculture.org.uk/

Hereford Museum
The Museum Resource and Learning Centre,
58 Friar Street
Hereford
Herefordshire, HR4 0AS
www.herefordshire.gov.uk/museums

The National Trust Wade Costume Collection
Snowshill Manor (stored at Berrington Hall)
Berrington Hall
Leominster, HR6 0DW
http://www.nationaltrustcollections.org.uk

The Olive Matthews Collection
Chertsey Museum
The Cedars,
33 Windsor Street,
Chertsey,
Surrey, KT16 8AT
http://chertseymuseum.org/

The Russell-Cotes Art Gallery and Museum
Russell Cotes Road
Bournemouth
BH1 3AA
http://russellcotes.com/

Symington Corsetry Collection
Leicestershire County Council
The Collections Resources Centre
Hayhill, Sileby Road
Barrow-Upon-Soar
Loughborough
Leicestershire, LE12 8LD
http://imageleicestershire.org.uk

Victoria and Albert Museum
The Clothworkers' Centre for the Study and Conservation of Textiles and Fashion.
Blythe House
23 Blythe Road
London, W14 0QX
http://www.vam.ac.uk/page/c/clothworkers-centre/

UK and US suppliers of pattern drafting and corsetry materials

UK

Vena Cava Design
PO Box 3597
Poole
BH14 9ZL
www.venacavadesign.co.uk

Devine Supplies
41 Manor Rd
South Benfleet
Benfleet
SS7 4BE
Tel: 01702 352500 or
01702 613101
https://devinesupplies.co.uk/

MacCulloch and Wallis
25-26 Poland St
Soho
London
W1F 8QN
Phone: 020 7629 0311
www.macculloch-wallis.co.uk

Morplan Ltd
56 Great Titchfield Street
Fitzrovia
London
W1W 7DF
Tel: 020 7636 1887
www.morplan.com/shop/en/morplan
Specialist pattern drafting equipment

Whaleys (Bradford) Ltd
Harris Court
Great Horton
Bradford, West Yorkshire
BD7 4EQ
Telephone: +44 (0) 1274 576718
http://www.whaleys-bradford.ltd.uk/

US

Richard the Thread
1960 S. La Cienega Blvd
Los Angeles
CA 90034
Tel: +1-310-837-4997
www.richardthethread.com

Farthingales
Linda Sparks
20 Monteith Ave
Stratford
ONTARIO
CANADA N5A 2P4
Tel: 1-519-275-2374
www.farthingales.on.ca

Corset Making Supplies
Delicious, LLC
212 E. Girard Ave
Philadelphia
PA 19125
www.corsetmaking.com
Tel: 215-413-8259

Bibliography and further reading

Bibliography

Arnold, J. (1985) *Patterns of Fashion: The Cut and Construction of Clothes for Men and Women c1560–1620*. London: Macmillan.

Ashelford, J. (1996) *The Art of Dress. Clothes through History 1500 to 1914*. London: National Trust Enterprises Ltd.

Warren, P. and Nicol, S. (2013) *Foundations of Fashion, the Symington Corsetry Collection 1860–1990*. Leicestershire: Leicestershire County Council.

Waugh, N. (2000) *Corsets and Crinolines*. New York: Routledge/ Theatre Arts Book.

Further reading

Barrington, M. (2015) *Stays and Corsets: Historical Patterns Translated for the Modern Body*. New York: Focal Press.

Benson, Elain and Esten, John (1996) *Un-Mentionables: A Brief History of Underwear*. New York: Simon and Schuster Editions.

Fontanel, B. (1997) *Support and Seduction A History of Corsets and Bras*. New York: Harry N. Abrams.

Kyoto Costume Institute. (2002). *Fashion – A History from the 18th to the 20th Century – the Collection of the Kyoto Costume Institute*. Koln: Benedikt Taschen.

Lynn, E. (2010) *Underwear Fashion in Detail*. London: V&A Publishing.

North, S. and Tiramani, J. Ed (2011) *Seventeenth Century Women's Dress Patterns. Book One*. London: V&A Publications.

Ribeiro, A. (2003) *Dress and Morality*. New York: Berg Publishers Ltd.

Salen, J. (2008) *Corsets: Historical Patterns and Techniques*. London: Batsford.

Sparks, L. (2005) *The Basics of Corset Building. A Handbook for Beginners*. New York: St. Martin's Press.

Steele, V. (2001) *The Corset: A Cultural History*. London: Yale University Press.